THE GIRL IN THE RURAL FAMILY

THE GIRL
IN THE RURAL FAMILY

By

NORA MILLER, B.S., M.S.

VIRGINIA AGRICULTURAL AND
HOME ECONOMICS EXTENSION SERVICE

CHAPEL HILL

THE UNIVERSITY OF NORTH CAROLINA PRESS

1935

Copyright, 1935, by
The University of North Carolina Press

DURHAM, N. C., AND BOUND BY L. H. JENKINS, INC., RICHMOND, VA.

INSPIRED BY

TWO THOUSAND GIRL FRIENDS

AND

DEDICATED TO

MRS. FRANCES SHUTTLEWORTH

PREFACE

Association with teachers, ministers, home demonstration agents, rural rehabilitation supervisors, nurses, social workers, and others interested in improving the quality of family life in rural areas has convinced the writer that there is a place for a book describing in simple language the routine of living of the people of different rural occupations in the South. The facts used in this volume were collected by the author. Some of them were analyzed statistically but figures have been used merely as a basis for determining the prevalence of certain characteristics found in the various sections described. The status of the out-of-school girl is discussed more in detail than that of other members of the family.

It is hoped that this information will be helpful to educational and social workers in general, and especially to those interested in developing a program for young women from the time they leave school till they are established in business or in homes of their own.

N. M.

April, 1935.

TABLE OF CONTENTS

	PAGE
PREFACE	vii

CHAPTER

I. INTRODUCTION 3

II. THE DEPENDENT FAMILY......................... 6
Physical Surroundings—Outside Relations—Routine of Living—The Out-of-School Girl.

III. THE MOUNTAIN FARM FAMILY..................... 15
Physical Surroundings—Outside Relations—Routine of Living—The Out-of-School Girl.

IV. THE SOFT COAL MINE FAMILY..................... 27
The Family Financial System—Outside Relations—Routine of Living—The Out-of-School Girl.

V. THE COTTON FARM FAMILY........................ 39
Physical Surroundings—Family Finances—Outside Relations—Routine of Living—The Out-of-School Girl.

VI. THE TOBACCO FARM FAMILY...................... 53
Physical Surroundings—The Food Supply—Outside Relations—Routine of Living—The Out-of-School Girl.

VII. THE FISHING COMMUNITY FAMILY................ 65
The House—Income and Food Supply—Outside Relations—Routine of Living—The Out-of-School Girl.

VIII. THE POTATO FARM FAMILY........................ 74
Physical Surroundings—Income and Food Supply—Outside Relations—Routine of Living—The Out-of-School Girl.

IX. THE SUPERIOR RURAL FAMILY..................... 85
Physical Surroundings—Outside Relations—Routine of Living—The Out-of-School Girl.

X. INSTRUCTING THE GIRL IN THE FAMILY............. 93
Club Work among Tobacco Farm Girls—Club Work among Coal Mine Girls—Club Work among Potato Farm Girls—Suggestions for Projects and Programs.

THE GIRL IN THE RURAL FAMILY

CHAPTER I
INTRODUCTION

UNTIL THE TIME of the World War, the girl in the rural family grew up with the idea of establishing a home of her own at an early age. She received training in the mechanics of housekeeping while helping her mother with the routine of work. She usually began her married life in the neighborhood of her home and had her mother's help for a few months thereafter. Such training, however, has become inadequate in view of certain social and economic changes which have in turn brought about changes in the attitude toward family life.

During the years following the World War, commercial amusements and public eating places diverted the interest in the home as the center of social activity. Moreover, when the business world opened its doors on a large scale to women, those who were left at home envied those who went out into the world and held positions. And furthermore, during the years of business expansion many girls aspired, and were often urged by their parents, to get enough education to earn their own money. Many families who had little regard for higher education sent their daughters to college with the idea that the girls would thereby be able to make more than had been spent on them.

These forces leading the girl into new centers of interest and activity were, and continue to be, broadening and good if she can get a job which pays well and can establish herself socially in a new environment. But unhappy situations often arise when she leaves her home environment and can not find her place in other groups of people. Girls with financial obligations to their families often have difficulty trying to meet these and at the same time maintain the standards of living which their new situations in life demand. The average, the unexceptional girl, therefore, probably has a better chance to adjust herself to life as an adult if she stays in her own environment and improves herself gradually, than she does if she goes to a new one for a while and then has to return home because there is no place in the business world for her.

With the decline of business, resulting in diminished incomes, in a decreasing number of jobs open to women, and in an increasing amount of leisure time, many girls have had to return to their rural homes and fewer have had the opportunity to leave them. This situation has tended to restore the home to its former important place as the center of a woman's interest. Increasing recognition of the importance of the home is shown by the fact that the 1930 census listed homemaking as a business, while in former years the homemaker was considered unemployed. The home of today must therefore undergo a number of changes in order to accept the responsibilities which have been returned to it.

Until recently the rural girl who was out of school had received little attention from social workers. A survey made in 1930 in one county included in this study showed that there were seventy-eight girls over fifteen years old out of school and a hundred and sixty of the same age in school. The increasing number of girls who are practically idle for several years after leaving school has been brought to the attention of educators, and effort is being made toward working out a type of education which will meet their needs.

A well-planned, semi-formal program of education can be very valuable in guiding girls from the time they leave school until they are established in homes of their own. The value which any given girl can get from such a program will naturally depend upon the elements affecting her intimate life—her native ability, ambitions, and desires, her past experiences and contacts, her prejudices, handicaps, and personal philosophy of life. Since these elements vary with individuals within a group as well as with different groups, a program for any one group must be broad enough to meet the needs of each individual in it. Provision must likewise be made for guidance on personal problems when a girl shows a desire for it.

One of the best ways of understanding the elements which affect a girl's private life and the problems which confront her is through a study of her home life. In the following chapters the family and community life of people in six southern rural occupations is described. The status of the out-of-school girl is stressed in each case. Descriptions of the Dependent Family, Chapter II, and of the Superior Family, Chapter IX, show the common characteristics of these families regardless of their location. The order in which the other chapters are arranged represents no effort on the part of the writer to rate the families or to compare them one with another. The recommendations of Chapter X are based on several years' experience of the writer in working with out-of-school girls.

CHAPTER II

THE DEPENDENT FAMILY

There are in every community a few families who cannot maintain themselves independently, who fail even to provide adequately such physical necessities as food, shelter, and clothing. Low mentality, illness or other physical handicaps, drunkenness, death of the wage earner, or lack of a feeling of responsibility may place a family in the dependent or public charge class. During the present crisis a great many responsible families have been temporarily placed in this class, but the characteristics here described apply only to those commonly known as the "old chronics." They may live in a rented house or one which was once theirs but is now so heavily mortgaged that their ownership will be of short duration even if the mortgage holder keeps the taxes paid.

Such a family farms a little in a crude way and the man may do a few odd jobs, such as working gardens or mowing lawns for people in the community. Other members may do day labor and in some cases domestic servant work. However, earnings are not regular and are too small to maintain a home. Aid in the form of grocery orders, clothes, and medical care from a charitable agency is usually provided periodically or regularly for a definite period. Probably the parents hesitated to accept this assistance at first; after once receiving charity, however, they not only accept the relief but expect it, unless encouragement to return to the state of self-support comes from an outside source along with the direct relief.

PHYSICAL SURROUNDINGS

The house is too small for the health and comfort of the family. Beds are scattered all over the house except in one small room which is used for cooking and eating. The house is in need of repair. Often the necessary improvements could be made with little or no cost if the man had initiative enough to use hammer and nails. Ashes and soot usually accumulate in the stoves or fireplace till they will not work satisfactorily.

Sleeping quarters are unattractive and often dirty. Household pests thrive. Methods of controlling these insects usually damage the furniture. Chair bottoms are partly torn, dresser drawer knobs are off, and the other furniture is in a dilapidated condition. The floors are bare and greasy and walls are smoked. Calendars from local grocery stores hang on the walls, usually two or three deep on a nail and dating back for several years.

Kitchen furnishings are inadequate for civilized living. Cooking utensils are few and serving dishes are not used. Plates and cups are of very cheap china and last for only a short time. Sometimes there are not enough of these or of knives and forks to set the table for the entire family. Very little food is produced at home and practically none is saved for out of season use. Incidentally, the diet is limited to bread and meat, with a few vegetables in season.

Water and wood are brought in as they are needed. The woman or oldest girl may make two or three trips to the well or pump and woodpile while a meal is being prepared. The fuel is cut as it is used, so that cooking when the wood is wet is not easy. The family laundry is done in the kitchen or yard, usually in the yard near the well.

The water bucket, a tin or zinc pail holding about two gallons, a dipper, and a tin wash basin are kept on a small table or box in the kitchen. The family towel hangs near by. Most of the bathing and water drinking are done here.

The physical surroundings of the dependent family indicate shiftlessness, lack of a sense of responsibility to the community to meet a respectable standard of living, and little regard for order and beauty.

Outside Relations

The family has no definite attachment to the community other than through the school. Any little excuse is used to keep a child at home a day or two or to take him out for the term unless compulsory attendance is enforced. The children are as a rule dirty and poorly dressed so that they are shunned by other children. They have trouble in adjusting themselves to the classroom routine and in mingling with other children on the playground. When a problem of discipline arises the child tells his story to his parents and they think the teacher is wrong. This attitude brings about more problems for the teacher. It is not uncommon for a child from a dependent home to be in a class two or three grades below the other children of his age. The parents occasionally attend a school program when the children are to take a part.

The man goes to the grocery store occasionally and joins the neighborhood men in condemning the government and blaming somebody for hard times. The woman visits a relative occasionally. The boy likely joins the roughest crowd in the community for liquor parties and gambling if he can get a few pennies to start with.

The family does not attend church and the minister calls only in case of serious illness or death in the family.

When a member of the family is ill, the others want the doctor every time there is any indication of a change. However, they are slow to carry out his instructions and often substitute homemade remedies which the neighbors suggest in place of the physician's prescription. No thought is given to paying the doctor for his services.

The substantial people condemn the members of such a family for their state of existence. Likely they aided them when they first fell below the poverty line and will still do so in case of extreme emergency, yet they give them little encouragement to rise above the poverty-stricken condition. If they are left in poverty and with broken self-respect for a period of years, they will have no desire to improve and the children will grow up with the attitude that it is quite all right for the public to support them.

ROUTINE OF LIVING

There are seven or eight children in the family. The children are not wanted and the woman constantly complains of the hard lot of having them. However, after they arrive they are welcome. And when a man has got the habit of asking for charity, he considers a large number of dependent children an asset.

There is little system or order in the family. Common courtesies and simple rules which enable people to live together with a minimum amount of friction are practically unknown. Physical punishment is the accepted way of disciplining the family and it is not always limited to the children. The parents frequently clash over the punishment of a child and take opposite views in the presence of the emotionally upset child, leaving him to suffer the pain from corporal punishment with no idea of the way in which he is expected to behave under similar conditions in the future.

The woman gets out of bed at about daybreak and calls all members of the household. She and the oldest girl cook breakfast. Usually the girl washes the dishes and sets the table while the woman prepares the bread and meat. The members of the family come in one at a time and eat without regard for formality or table manners. The dishes are usually arranged in a disorderly way on an oilcloth cover and the chairs or benches are brought to their places as each person starts to the table. If any children go to school on the bus, they must put some of the bread and meat cooked for breakfast into a paper bag or newspaper for lunch and rush to the road. In spite of the fact that the family gets up early the disorderly routine causes a great deal of time to be wasted and it is hard for one to get to a place on time. The rest of the housework is done in a haphazard way with much complaining by those who have to do the various jobs because nobody else will do them.

The father gets a great deal of pleasure from chewing tobacco and he teaches his sons the same habit as soon as they are old enough to want to imitate him. Although money is scarce, a way is usually found to get this luxury. The man and boys do not like to help with errands around the house though the woman often asks them to get wood and water for cooking.

There is no regular storage place for clothes, and therefore after wash day each person must look over the house till he finds his own. The girls have no place to hang their dresses where they are protected from smoke and insects; so they must be folded and placed in a disorderly drawer to be moved by other members of the family if they go searching for an article of wearing apparel, or a hammer, for either may be found in the drawer. If the girls have enough pride to want to appear neatly dressed it is almost impossible for them to do so in such a disorderly house.

Profane language and immodesty in the family are common. Lack of privacy, and low ideals are often responsible for immoral practices among young children. They are not taught to respect property rights within the family and they often have no regard for that which does not belong to them in the community. Abuse of the schoolhouse and other public property is prevalent. Petty theft which grows to the extent that it requires legal action is common among the children. However, going to jail is not especially embarrassing to the family that has lost its pride and feeling of independence.

If a child is sentenced to a corrective institution, the parents rejoice that he is to have some discipline, but they soon use every possible means of getting him paroled. When he returns after a year or two, he is usually less able to adjust himself to the community than he was before leaving the home he must return to.

The parents do not want the children to belong to community organizations. Sometimes they are afraid that the children will know more than they do or become critical of them; and often they see no need of play or other recreation. They consider the children as their personal property just as they do livestock, and think they should be around to do any work that must be done.

The dependent family has an inferiority complex. They frequently blame "bad luck" for their fate and take for granted that some way will be provided for their existence whether they put forth an effort or not. While there is food in sight for one day there is no worry. If any surplus money is on hand it may be spent for beads, toys for the children, or tobacco to save for future use. Clothes are not cleaned or mended as they need attention, and so they do not last long. When a sufficient wardrobe is provided for the family to make a decent appearance in public the best garments may be worn everyday, so that within two or three weeks the children could not go to public places if they wanted to.

Crowded living quarters, which are trying even in well organized families, make people with no system or organization naturally nervous and irritable. If a child prepares any lessons at home he must do it by a poor light in the room where the disorderly family is arguing and complaining, but if he does not pass his grade the parents often blame the teacher.

In case of serious illness or death in the family a great emotional display is made. Kindness of neighbors and the coming of strangers who may offer assistance excite the family.

This family is not only a financial but a social liability to a community. The children have a poor physical start and no recognized place in social life. The perpetuation of families below the poverty line hinders the progress of any community.

The Out-of-School Girl

The girl quits school at fourteen or fifteen years of age before completing the grammar grades. She had to stay at home to help with the work a day or two each week during her last year in school. She was conscious of her poor clothes and general unattractiveness. She had few friends in school and the other girls in the class were two or three years younger than she. She had little encouragement at home to continue her studies and the parents were glad when she decided just to stay at home. She had more schooling than her parents and they think they had enough to get along with.

The mother likes to show her authority by ordering the girl around and dictating the way she is to do the housework. She refuses to let her try out new methods of cooking or cleaning. Housework is boresome to the girl as well as to her mother, and both constantly complain about having it to do. There is no companionship between the mother and daughter in work or play.

The girl does not get medical and dental care when she needs it. Physical defects may depress the girl to the extent that she loses any ambition she might have acquired at school. These with the lack of clothes and money are strong barriers in the way of her making satisfactory adjustments to life as a woman.

The girl has little social life and no recreation. If she learned to enjoy reading while in school she has nothing to read. If she learned to appreciate music she has no opportunity to hear good music, and she has no profitable hobby. She has little chance to improve herself even if she wanted to.

When she becomes interested in a boy and he shows her any attention, the parents raise an objection. Naturally for a boy to be interested in such a girl other than for the physical attraction she has for him, he must be on the same social level or beneath her. The family usually recognizes the worthlessness of a boy regardless of their own position. The girl must slip around to see him to avoid added family clashes. Her chances to marry a boy who will earn a living for her are few.

When this girl does marry, the people of the community condemn her for the foolish step but she has nothing else to look forward to. Unless some educational institution can interest her in preparing for the job of homemaking she can only copy the home she came from. While the leading people criticize the girl for marrying young they offer her no alternative to adjust herself to accepted social standards of the community and to find a purpose in living.

CHAPTER III

THE MOUNTAIN FARM FAMILY

THE FARMER of the Appalachian Mountains in the southwestern part of Virginia owns or has a long time lease on about twenty acres of rugged and rocky land. This is located on a ridge or in a hollow large enough for a dozen or more such farms. Practically all the necessary food and feed are grown on the farm. The small cash crops are tobacco, corn, livestock, apples, peaches, potatoes, and berries. The man depends on a day or two of public work in the coal mines or on the county roads each month for extra cash. Farm products are generally of a poor quality and hard to get to market. The growing season is short. Therefore, little cash is available for the family to live on.

PHYSICAL SURROUNDINGS

The house is small. It was started with one room and a lean-to and other rooms were added as the family increased. It rests on an open foundation of native rocks. The house is unpainted both inside and out. The inside walls are darkened by age or smoke and partly covered with meaningless pictures and old calendars. In some cases the entire house is papered with magazine covers and newspapers.

There are beds in all the rooms except a small one which is used for cooking and eating. If the house is large enough the girls and boys occupy separate rooms and the small children share the one with the parents. The house is heated by one fireplace located in the parents' bedroom. The milk churn has a place by the fireside during the winter each day till churning time. The windows are small but attractively curtained. The furniture is sturdy and often unfinished. Floors are bare and subject to weekly scrubbings. There is little regard for order in the arrangement of the house. Clothes and wraps are hung on nails on the walls throughout. The shotgun is in a rack provided for it over the door in the room with the fireplace.

The water supply is a near-by spring or a well in the yard. The woman does not object to taking the water up a hill when the spring is several hundred feet below the house. Wood is cut on the farm or coal is dug from a small mine in the neighborhood. The fuel and kindling are piled in the yard and chopped up as they are needed. The yard is bare except for summer flowers in conspicuous beds and a few overgrown rose bushes. The woodpile and clothesline are visible from the front entrance. The yard is kept free from leaves and rubbish by regular sweeping with brooms made from small branches of dogwood and other trees with strong limbs.

The cow is the most cherished family possession. The woman milks and feeds her twice a day, calls her by name, keeps her clean and free from annoying insects, and looks out for her welfare in general. Milk and corn meal, which is ground weekly at a neighborhood grist mill, are the staple foods. Since the growing season is very short, a great deal of the year-round food supply must necessarily be stored. The people are clever at making apple butter, pickling beans, making sauerkraut, and banking cabbage. A little fruit is canned or preserved, though the quality is poor. The stored food does not provide a balanced diet for every day in the year, but the family does not go hungry, and the general health is fair.

Life in the mountain farmhouse is plain, crowded, clean, and individual. The man is proud of his home but sees no necessity for modern conveniences, sanitary facilities, paint, or a sodded lawn. The woman says nothing about improvements for she sees no way to get them. She does consider it her duty, however, to keep the house clean and the family well fed.

OUTSIDE RELATIONS

The ridge or hollow is an isolated neighborhood made up of from a dozen to fifty families. This area composes to a great extent the known world to the inhabitants. Everybody is known by his first name and family skeletons are generally discussed. Neighbors who are on speaking terms visit each other frequently. It is customary to open the front door and walk in without calling or knocking. It is all right for one to stay for a meal if he happens to be in a neighbor's house when it is ready to be served. Neighborhood quarrels are ordinary happenings. Sometimes several families will refuse to be on speaking terms with several other families over a petty grievance involving two people. However, the grievances soon disappear and other families in turn quarrel and make up.

There are two churches in the community. One is a mission center with an outside worker supported by some Protestant denomination. The other is a primitive and unorganized church, requiring simply conformance to a narrow ritual for membership, and depending on emotional appeal for its followers. The primitive church disapproves of a religious education program and Sunday-School. The ministers are selected from the congregation and serve without training. Long services on Saturday and Sunday are the leading social events. Baptizings are important affairs. Often funerals are held at the cemetery several weeks after the burial. Existing superstitions cause a great many conflicts between parents and children when the latter learn to reason out things for themselves and cannot accept the teachings of their fathers' religion. The minister visits a great deal and interprets current history to the people with whom he comes in contact.

The children go to the two- or three-room school till they complete the grades taught or get tired of going. The parents and the children do know how to read and write but they do not have a high regard for book learning.

Seasonal neighborhood workings are enjoyable social events. One family invites a dozen or more other families to the working on a set day. The host family provides an elaborate dinner with several kinds of meat and a variety of cakes and pies for all who come. The men clear land, pile brush, or do other heavy work, and the women quilt. Usually enough work is accomplished to pay for the food that was bought, and everybody has as much fun as if he had gone to a picnic. There may be a half dozen such gatherings in a neighborhood in one season. Prospective office holders do not refuse an opportunity for contact with voters if they get an invitation to such a gathering. They may not join in the work but they are there to chat with the men at dinner.

Apple butter making is another social event. No efficient housekeeper is without several gallons of this sweet when winter comes. The making of apple butter is one job which the man is glad to help with. A large brass or copper kettle and a stirring paddle are the necessary equipment. The afternoon before the apple butter is to be made the woman and several neighbors work long hours peeling apples in readiness for the event. By daybreak the next morning a fire is built around the kettle in the yard and the apples with a definite proportion of sugar are added. The stirring paddle has a handle several feet long so that the person using it can stand away from the hot fire which is kept around the kettle all the time it is supposed to be boiling. The neighbors gather to talk, to assist with the stirring, and to help keep the fire mended. This process continues for eight or nine hours. The finished product is put into unsterilized jars and sealed. If it molds, the housewife accepts the fact as a matter of course. Her responsibility is to have the required number of gallons in the pantry. Other families in turn announce their apple butter cooking days and the social affairs continue till late in the fall.

The man goes to the closest grocery store once or twice a week and buys such articles as tobacco, matches, and small groceries. He goes to the closest village a few times a year and buys plow tools and clothes for the family. However, most of the clothing is purchased from mail order houses or at second hand sales held at mission centers. The woman goes to the village once in two or three years.

The teacher is invited to spend the night in various homes once during the school term. If she accepts she must sleep with one or two of the girls. She likely eats her meals alone or with the older children.

Most mountain people are musical and the boys play stringed instruments. The neighborhood boys gather at various homes and play their instruments. Where people do not belong to the church they utilize the music for square dancing. The girls sometimes gather with the boys and sing while they play. The young people often join the adults in singing at church, but musical instruments are not permitted in the loosely organized churches.

The woman is a practical nurse for her family and the women in the neighborhood when they need her assistance. The midwife is an important person in the community and a friend to every family. She teaches the women simple principles of home nursing and assists them in carrying out a doctor's orders when one is called. Since the services of a doctor are very expensive in such isolated communities, the midwife takes care of baby cases, and home remedies are used for minor ailments.

The family once had a second hand car but it had to be discarded several years ago because of lack of money for the upkeep. No one regards it a hardship to walk three or four miles to a social gathering or to a store. Some of the ambitious young people walk fourteen miles a day to high school.

Young people begin their courting at school and continue it at church and social gatherings in homes. When a boy and a girl go together a few times, the adults tease them and encourage the romance. Frequently such interference leads the couple to go together to the exclusion of other possible mates just because the public expects them to do so.

A wedding is a community event whether it is a quiet affair away from home or an elaborate one with many guests. People of the neighborhood gather and demand treats from the bridegroom just as soon as they can see him after the wedding. He may be subjected to bodily harm by mischievous boys if he refuses. It is not uncommon for him to have to buy ten dollars' worth of drinks and candy to satisfy a demanding crowd.

The family has a great many contacts with the people of the immediate neighborhood but very little association with people from other communities and towns.

ROUTINE OF LIVING

The man is the head of the family and he is proud of his position. He markets the products, pays the bills, makes the purchases, directs the farm work, and dictates to his wife and children regarding their work and play. He regards his wife neither as his equal nor as a weak being who needs protecting from the hardships of life. He does not shield her from drudgery and he is perfectly willing to leave home to keep from seeing her draw water to wash the clothes or cut wood to cook a meal if he is not in the humor to do this work. The man pays little attention to the everyday courtesies which men of refinement observe when in the presence of ladies, such as removing the hat or holding a door for a woman to enter.

The woman and children have little money to spend since they must ask the man for it or ask him to buy the necessary articles which they want. The man's tobacco is the first necessity in the family. The man expects everybody around the house to cater to him and provide him with physical comforts. He wants his meals on time, and his appetite is limited in the choice of vegetables. He constantly complains about high taxes, low farm prices, and hard times. He toils hard in the field for long hours during the crop season but he does little work during the rest of the year. He sits around the country store or goes fishing a great deal of the time.

He has few clothes and does not mind wearing them soiled or patched. The woman tries to foresee his wants and to keep him in as good humor as she can by providing the things which will please him.

The woman lives a life of physical labor and drudgery. Her faith in a reward in the next world for sufferings and work well done on earth is about all the encouragement or incentive which she has for living. She rises before daybreak in winter and by daylight in summer to begin her never finished household toils. She cooks and serves the meals to the members of the family as they come to the table one or two at a time. After the others have eaten she eats her meal alone while standing. Often she takes her food from the boilers and saucepans without using a plate. She cares for the milk after milking the cow, and cares for the chickens and pig if there is one. She sweeps the yards, scrubs the floors, washes, irons, mends, sews, works the garden and flowers, and helps with the hoeing and harvesting of the crop.

The woman has little social life or even conversation with the various members of the family. Conversation with neighbors is frequently neighborhood gossip. She may have a hobby of quilt making or rug making. The mountain woman has a deep appreciation of color harmonies and often creates attractive and artistic articles from ordinary materials. The woman seldom reads or gets new thoughts. She is extremely jealous of her husband and thinks that other women want him. This narrow and monotonous life often leads her to be irritable and to have a nagging habit.

The girls help the mother with all the housework. They learn to do the various jobs as she does them. She has definite standards of cleanliness and requires them to meet these. The girl is expected to be a good housekeeper so she takes a little pride in the work at an early age. When she begins having dates at about fourteen years of age her interest in a clean house and yard grows.

The parents instinctively object to the first two or three dates but finally agree to the daughter's having company. They provide the best clothes they can for her. They hold her to strict rules regarding bedtime hours and having a chaperon when she goes with a young man. However, the girls are shrewd enough to conform to these rules in theory but to have as much freedom as modern girls usually take.

The girl knows little about the biological facts of life. Often her knowledge is covered with superstitions which not only depress her but endanger her health. When a girl is preparing for her wedding she may ask the local midwife to tell her the facts which she wants the truth about. It worries a mother to think her daughter knows anything about the physical facts before she is married.

The boys help with the labor on the farm, taking more of the heavy labor as they grow older. They fish with the father and accompany him to the store occasionally. The boys get their spending money by asking the father for it till they are twenty-one years of age; then they have a definite share in the crop or begin farming for themselves. They go to church, to parties, to musical gatherings in the neighborhood, and to the village a few times a year.

The community and the home have a definite set of rules for measuring morality. The minister is instrumental in making these rules and the older people attempt to carry them out. Parents frequently give the children moral lectures and try to keep them from dancing, playing cards, and taking part in other activities which are not accepted in the church. When a young man calls on a girl the parents remind him that it is bedtime if he does not voluntarily leave at an early hour. The wiles of men are constantly kept before the girls, and they are warned every few days by the mother of the dangers which they face. The boys get similar lectures about women from the father.

Family life is to a great extent unorganized and social contacts are few. Therefore few ideals of parents are passed on to the children other than those regarding moral standards. Blood kin is the strongest bond that unites the people. There may be discord within a family, but if a member is attacked by an outside enemy the entire family will die for a brother or cousin if necessary.

The members of the family are generally poorly groomed and the men have little regard for cleanliness of body or clothes. A dirty collar is quite all right if the man has worn the shirt only for a week. Lack of privacy and a convenient water supply in the home probably has something to do with this attitude. Separate sleeping garments are not generally used and bed linens are used for a long time without laundering.

The mountain farm family recognizes no social classes either in the community or out. However, there are people with whom they do not care to associate, but each family feels itself as good as the best people in the state. A rather amusing but truthful experience regarding a Christmas gift to a janitor illustrates the fact that social classes are not recognized. Two college trained women doing social work in a mountain county with headquarters in the courthouse presented the janitor, a man past sixty years of age, with a tie and a card of thanks for his services as a Christmas remembrance. His wife became indignant and accused the old man of prolonging his work at the courthouse after those women began working there.

THE OUT-OF-SCHOOL GIRL

The mountain farm girl left school at the age of fourteen or fifteen when she had completed the sixth or seventh grade in grammar school. Her only thought of the future was to help with the work at home for a year or two and then marry a boy in the community. Since she knew the fundamentals of housekeeping before she left school, she had little adjustment to make to the routine of work at home.

The mother feels that it is her duty to train the girl to be a good housekeeper although her methods are crude. Social workers sometimes find mothers resenting their teaching girls to cook or sew in a modern way. They regard it the divine calling of the mother to train the daughter in housewifery. However, the girl is eager to learn modern methods although she cannot use them in her mother's home. If the girl learns better table manners or even a standard way of setting the table, she may be ridiculed by her older brothers and even her parents for trying to put them into practice at home.

The girl, like her mother, works in the field during the crop season and does the work at the house besides. She works as a day laborer both at the house and in the field. She gets money for clothes and other necessities as the father feels that he can spare it. She makes quilts or does fancy work as a hobby and in preparation for marriage. Although mother and daughter work together on these things there is little sociability between the two. The girl seeks companionship with other girls and talks over her private affairs with them. This girl has a very narrow and often uninteresting life and looks at it from the viewpoint of years of sacrificial service with a reward in the next world just as her mother has done.

She will quite likely marry a boy with whom she has grown up. She had a year or two more in school than he did but his contacts with the outside world through occasional visits to the village or county seat will soon raise him above her educational level. The mother will be near to nurse her when she is sick and when the children come.

Although the girl has a narrow and uninteresting life she is generally contented. She accepts marriage and homemaking as her calling and puts her best self into it. She has little opportunity to make a better home than her mother but she will try to live above criticism and make that home a credit to the community.

CHAPTER IV

THE SOFT COAL MINE FAMILY

THE COAL DIGGER with his wife and seven or eight children live in a frame house located in a mining town. From seventy-five to three hundred families make up the mining town. The houses are built for individual families though two are often joined at one end. After the coal digger is hired by a firm and has passed the necessary physical examination, he selects an empty house which he can afford and arranges with the company for it. He must select a house on a street designated for coal diggers. If he gets a promotion he can move on another street and into a better house. A man's job determines the social standing of the family as well as the place of residence.

Rent is paid by the room. Usually the family rents as many bedrooms as can be afforded and an extra one for the kitchen and dining room. The mother's room is usually the sitting room as well as a bedroom. Three or four people occupy one room. There is a porch and small yard which serve as living quarters in the summer. A few flowers may be grown in the yard.

The house is ceiled and painted both inside and out. The color is that used as a standard by the company. It is usually gray or brown. Paint is bought in large quantities and used for the entire town. The floors are bare and get weekly scrubbings.

Water, fuel, and lights are furnished by the company and paid for out of the pay roll allowance at a flat rate with the rent. A faucet in the back yard supplies the water for all household purposes. The coal is kept in the back yard also. Coal is used for all heating and cooking purposes. Laundry is done on the back porch. Each room is wired for an electric light suspended from the center of the ceiling.

The furniture is cheap and fancy. It stands only a few years of wear if it is moved two or three times. Bright-colored iron beds and golden oak dressers are the usual pieces. A large Victrola and an expensive coal range bought on the installment plan are family possessions if the payments were finished before the decline of the mining business. The table is covered with oilcloth. Serving dishes, silver, and cooking utensils are cheap and last only for a short time.

There is little system or order in the house. Freshly ironed clothes, winter coats, hats, torn pictures, calendars, and other articles hang at random on the walls. A shelf in the mother's bedroom is used for the medicine chest, shaving equipment, match box, family comb and brush, soap dish, pencil and writing paper, and a half-dozen other pieces of small equipment. Laundry tubs are kept on the back porch and constantly annoy the men when they must walk around them. The housework can be done with little effort but it is a burden to the woman under the existing conditions. A great many family clashes arise over searches for personal articles.

The Family Financial System

The father is the only wage earner till the boys go to the mines at the age of eighteen if there is work for them. The girls may earn some money by domestic work after they are sixteen or seventeen years old. Every other Saturday is pay day. Two weeks' pay is always held in reserve. Scrip may be drawn on this during the period between pay days. This is accepted as cash at the company store. House rent, fuel, water and lights, and medical fees are deducted before scrip is issued. The scrip can be used by all members of the family. All wages which have not been taken up in scrip are paid the man in cash on the regular pay day.

It is customary to spend the money as it is earned. Very little, if any, is saved or invested in a money-making enterprise. The company carries compensation insurance on the worker. If he is killed while on duty, the family receives a monthly check for two years after the death. If the man is injured while on duty, he receives compensation till he is able to return to work or for a stated period.

Outside Relations

The mining town is a private community owned by the coal company employing the inhabitants. The superintendent of the mine is the mayor of the town. The policeman is appointed and paid by the company. Other officers are employees of the company and serve only part time. One or more doctors work on a salary for the company. They are paid from the medical fees deducted from each man's wages. The fee entitles the man and his family to medical treatment and hospital care as they are needed. An extra charge is made for maternity cases.

The children attend the public school located in the town in a building furnished by the company. However, the school is a part of the county system. The boys will not finish the grammar grades and the girls will quit before or immediately after entering high school.

The children go to Sunday-School and the parents

attend church services occasionally. The churches of one or more denominations are important institutions. The minister lives in a company owned house and buys his groceries at the company store. In some cases his salary is paid through the company's office from small deductions from the pay roll of the various workers. However, the salary is generally donated by the members as in any other community. The minister takes the lead in most of the social and recreational activities of the young people, if there are any. The minister visits his members several times a year, conducts funerals, marries a few of the young people, and leads the religious education program in the community or his part of it.

There is a company owned and operated theater with movies one or two nights a week. The children go regularly and the mother and father go a few times a year.

The company store supplies the food and plain clothes as well as confections, cold drinks, and seasonal novelties. It is customary for the family to patronize the company store regardless of the prices. And as scrip can be used in the place of cash, the family has no objections to this custom. The post office is located in one corner of the store or in an adjoining part of the same building. The store is a great social center. The men congregate on the porch to talk and chew tobacco. The women visit while doing their shopping inside.

Peddlers or solicitors are not permitted to canvass a town or call on a family without a permit in writing from the superintendent of the mine. When a stranger must ask for directions for finding a particular family he goes to the policeman and explains the purpose of his errand. If the visit is strictly social the policeman is courteous to the stranger; otherwise he may refuse to locate the family till the order is given from the superintendent.

The children congregate in the neighborhood yards or on near-by vacant lots. The children have frequent disagreements which lead to quarrels between the mothers. It is not uncommon for two children to have a disagreement or fist fight which attracts the attention or arouses the anger of the mothers. While they are arguing or debating in an unpleasant way whose fault caused the fight, the children have made friends and gone to another yard to play. Most of the quarrels among women grow out of harmless childhood scraps.

When the boys are eleven or twelve years old they discard back-yard play and form gangs of a dozen or more boys who meet on vacant lots and plan their own activities. The older boys have organized baseball teams and baseball is the leading sport among the young ones. However, the small boys often plan activities of an almost criminal nature. The girls have cliques which decrease in size at the age when those of the boys increase. The man belongs to a lodge or secret order which meets once or twice a month.

The man and woman grew up on neighboring farms in a near-by hollow or on a mountain ridge a few miles away. They married when quite young and started their life as farmers. With the opening of vast coal fields they moved to the coal town and an experienced miner taught the man to dig coal. The family entered a new world, but many of the mountain characteristics remain with them.

ROUTINE OF LIVING

The household routine must be adjusted according to the man's working hours. If he is on the day shift he leaves home at about six o'clock in the morning and returns at about four in the afternoon. When he changes to the night shift he leaves at five in the afternoon and returns before six in the morning. His shift changes every other month. When the man must sleep in the daytime he wants the house to be quiet; so the children must play away from the house.

The woman rises at about five o'clock in the morning and makes the fires, then calls the man. She cooks breakfast by the time he is dressed and packs his lunch while he eats. The miner's lunch is a heavy meal and fried meats do not keep in the underground atmosphere, so special attention must be given to the selection of food. The company store carries individual cans of meats, fruits, and individually wrapped cakes. However, a regular lunch from these packs is expensive. The lunch pail has two compartments. The bottom holds two quarts of water for drinking and the carbide lamp. The top section holds the food and forms a cover for the water. The lunch must be eaten while the man relaxes from his heavy labor and while he stands in the mine, a lump of coal serving as a resting place for the pail. The lunch is planned to suit the man's appetite as far as the available money will permit and little regard is given to nutritional value.

After dynamiting coal and loading the broken pieces into cars for eight or more hours the man returns home very tired. His wife has his dinner or supper ready as soon as he washes a bit and changes his clothes. All the family seldom sit down to a meal together. After the evening meal the man joins his friends on the store porch or at another community gathering place and chats till early bedtime.

Once a year a first aid course is held in the town. Every miner is required to take it. Classes are held daily in off-duty hours for a week or more. A man's failure to take this course may cause him to lose his job. The course is taught by a trained worker whose duty it is to help decrease the number of accidents in mine work.

The man, like his father on the mountain farm, likes to let the world know that he is at the head of his family. However, verbal dictation is about the only way he has to exert this authority. The scrip system takes the family purse out of his hands. As he is away a great deal of the time, the woman necessarily has to handle the problems of disciplining the children. The man complains about the boy friends of the daughter and tells her they are beneath her. He drinks some and is cross with the daughter if she has a date when he is intoxicated. The mother is clever in keeping the daughter's secrets from him, however.

After the woman sees the husband off to work or to bed, if he worked at night, she serves breakfast to the children and gets them ready for school. She does the housework and does not want to be worried by teaching her daughters to do it. A great deal of her time is spent in looking for the small children as they wander away to play in neighborhood yards without telling her where they are going. Since she has no hobby or profitable pastime she really wants to do all the house work in order to be occupied. She sits on the porch and talks with neighbors sometimes, visits relatives who may live in the town, and keeps the family's clothes washed and mended. She does not belong to a church or civic organization for women because it is made up of the wives of the foremen and officials of the company and she does not feel at home with them.

The women are conscious of social classes in the town and try to stay within their crowd. As was stated before, the work of the man determines the social standing. It is hard for any woman besides the wife of the superintendent, store keeper, or other recognized official to hold an office in a woman's organization. The women will say, "Why should I follow Mrs. X when my husband has just as good a job as hers?"

Usually one day each week is designated as "Woman's Day" at the company store. This is a social event with the women as well as a shopping tour. They buy cloth and novelties for which they have no immediate use if there is more available scrip than they need for immediate necessities. The woman realizes that she will not get the cash if there is any on pay day. She knows, too, that her husband is likely to spend it for liquor; so she uses her share in scrip. The regular daily shopping for groceries is done by the children. There is one price and little choice in quality; so a young child can take the scrip and a note to the store and make a purchase just as well as his mother. Large orders are usually delivered by the company's truck.

The older boys and girls spend much of their time away from home. As the girls have little home responsibility, they spend a great deal of their time visiting friends who live in the neighborhood, and going to the store and post office. The boys often have gangs which are familiar with amateur criminal practices, and may pursue these till legal procedure is necessary. However, most of these boys just go unnoticed till they are old enough to work in the mines. In some cases the company supplies equipment for a baseball team of older boys. This is a real asset to the community since it not only employs the team but sets an example for the little boys.

There are a great many small children in the community and they have no supervised form of play. The many conflicts which arise cause the women to pity themselves for having to rear a family in such a crowded place. It is not uncommon to hear a woman say she wished she had no neighbors nearer than five or six miles. In that case freedom from children's conflicts is her idea of happiness.

The woman tries hard to provide for the physical comforts of her husband and children. She may cease to love her husband but she realizes her dependence on his pay check and the attitude of her mother toward the marriage vows, so she gives herself in sacrificial service to the family.

The family neither owns a home or feels any attachment to one. No family furniture or silver is collected which will be valuable for the sentiment attached to it, no money or property is accumulated to be inherited by the children, and the parents have no definite ideals which they feel responsible for instilling into the minds of the children. Therefore the main function of the family is to provide food and clothes in the boarding house fashion for the various members of the family as they are born and till they are grown.

The Out-of-School Girl

The coal digger's daughter got tired of going to school and stopped before or soon after she completed the grammar grades. She quit at the age of fourteen or fifteen.

The life of leisure which she saw the girls a year or two older enjoying appealed to her more than the responsibility of preparing lessons to please the teacher or to impress her classmates. The parents were willing for her to discontinue her studies because she had had more school advantages than they.

The girl helps her mother a little with the housework, but there is no responsibility attached to what she does. The mother had rather do the work herself than bother to teach the girl, and she would have more idle time on her hands if the daughter helped much with the household routine. The girl, therefore, spends much of her time with small cliques of girls in homes of the various members, and she goes to the post office two or three times a day. There she lingers and talks with the young people who are idle.

These cliques amuse themselves in various ways. They set their own moral standards which are sometimes not approved by the community. However, a girl cares little for the opinion of anybody outside of her own crowd. Telling questionable jokes may be an accepted pastime in the group, even when boys are present. This may be one of the many unwholesome activities of the group.

The girl may attend church occasionally, but like her mother she has an inferiority complex when it comes to taking an active part in an organization which includes people socially above her. So it is that the coal digger's daughter is a rather loosely attached person in the home and community. She has no responsibility in either. Naturally she has a great deal of idle time unless she is fortunate enough to find a job.

After growing tired of the idle life, if a girl has a real ambition, she may be able to get work as a maid in a home in a near-by town or small city. There she will earn enough money to support herself and have the advantage of living in a well-ordered home. There she will learn the modern technique of doing housework. She can visit her family occasionally and keep in touch with the friends in her community. Unless she does keep her friends, she may become very lonely for she has little chance to make new ones where she works. Occasionally several girls can find employment in the same city neighborhood and be company for each other. However, most of the opportunities for such work come to individual girls a few miles from the mining town.

The courtship of the girl begins usually before she leaves school, and her first serious love affair ends her interest in books. She goes with boys from her own town or from other mining communities, but seldom with one from the family of another occupation. The father thinks that no man is good enough to go with his daughter. Often when he is intoxicated and disgusted with himself, he scolds the girl about going with boys. He sees no reason for her to go with the "sorry" boys. The mother remembers that she was taught to regard marriage and making a home as her mission in life, so she encourages the girl to go with eligible young men. She helps her avoid scoldings by the father. He complains about the cost of clothing the girl and reminds her that she is old enough to be making her own living. She must accept his complaints in this matter just as she does those about the boys.

When she finally gets her father's consent to go with a boy without slipping around, she has no place to entertain him at home. If the boy has the use of a car, they must ride; and if he has no car, their courting must be done while wandering around the neighborhood. After a brief courtship, the girl will go to the county seat or to another county and be married. She knows little about doing housework and nothing about handling money. She can only try to copy the home she left. Inefficient as her mother was, she was better prepared to make a home than the daughter is. The girl has no interesting hobby or form of recreation which she can continue after marriage. Therefore, when the excitement of the new life is over, she may become bored with the routine of housekeeping.

CHAPTER V

THE COTTON FARM FAMILY

THE FAMILY here described owns a farm of about forty acres in north Louisiana. The small farm-owning family and the white tenants of the same community have similar living standards and the same family characteristics. All members work for long hours in the field during the crop season. The woman and girls labor over the housework the rest of the year. The cash income is small, and modern conveniences and luxuries are necessarily few. There are five or six children in the family.

PHYSICAL SURROUNDINGS

The residence is a one-story frame building with a square tin roof. It has four or five rooms and a front porch. The inside walls are sealed but usually neither papered nor painted. The foundation is formed of several rows of oak blocks eight or ten feet apart. The house is heated by a small sheet iron stove in one bedroom. Separate rooms are usually used for cooking and eating but there is a bed in the living room. The family usually sits in the bedroom with the stove in winter and on the porch in summer. There is no bathroom. The bathing facilities consist of a wash basin, water bucket, and towel kept on the porch for the men to wash their faces and hands before meals, and a pail of water and pan in the kitchen for other bathing. An open well in the front or side yard supplies water for the house and sometimes for the livestock. Wood is the fuel used for cooking and heating.

The furniture consists of iron beds, oak dressers,

poorly constructed tables, a sewing machine, a Victrola, and chairs which must be replaced every few years. The furniture is usually in need of repair. The floors are bare or partly covered with linoleum rugs. Expensive enlarged family portraits hang on the walls. Such equipment as china, linen, knives and forks, and bedclothes are of a poor quality and wear for a very short time. Oilcloth is used on the dining table except when there is a guest for a meal. Then a damask tablecloth and napkins are used. Vases and bowls are found on the shelves, but when cut flowers are brought into the house they are put in glasses or fruit jars.

The yard is bare except for a few scattered shrubs and annual flowers in rock bordered beds. The woodpile, doghouse, washpot, and clothesline are in the yard and can usually be seen from the road at the front. Children's play equipment is scattered over the yard. The barn, chicken house, "smokehouse" or meat-curing house are scattered at the sides and make an unsightly appearance. There is no place for storing farm equipment; so plows, shovels, and other implements can be seen scattered over the yard or under the house. Loss of these articles causes many unnecessary family clashes, and replacing them is expensive.

The family has a good vegetable garden in the spring and a turnip patch in the fall. A few quarts of vegetables are stored for winter use. A cow provides milk a part of each year. One or two hogs are raised for meat and lard. A few chickens which find their food around the barn furnish eggs and a little meat. A few eggs are sold. One horse or mule is kept for cultivating each twenty acres of land. The family once owned a car but had to discard it because of lack of cash for license and gasoline.

The family is usually permanently located though the man talks of moving every time the crop fails to meet his expectations. He excuses himself for not making improvements on the place by saying he is going to move within a year or two. This attitude on his part is provoking to the woman who wants an orchard and household conveniences.

Family Finances

Cotton is planted late in April and harvested from September till early November. The cotton is sold as it is harvested or shortly after the harvest season closes. A merchant extends credit to the farmer for food, feed, fertilizer, and plain clothes for the family. After the cotton is ginned, graded, and put in the warehouse, the farmer takes his cotton tickets or receipts to the merchant. The merchant sells the cotton when he considers the market right or when he must have some money for his business. After deducting the amount due for the store account, the merchant either pays the farmer the rest in cash or credits it to his account to be traded out in the future. The farmer seldom sees the bill of sale for his crop and he does not get an itemized account of his purchases. Sometimes ten years will pass without a checking of account to determine the status of the farmer's finances. The small farmer is as much under the domination of the merchant as the tenant is of his landlord. Very likely the merchant extended the man credit when he bought the farm, and if any money was borrowed on it later the loan was made through the merchant.

After the cultivation of the cotton is finished about the middle of July, the farmer has five or six weeks of leisure time before the harvest season begins. Then from late November till the first week in March he does little work on the farm. During prosperous times the farmer could get a day or two of public work each week during the time he was not needed in the crop. Now there is no public work for him, so the income is dependent on the sale of the cotton entirely.

The work of farm and home demonstration agents in getting the farmer to return to his forefathers' practice of growing enough food at home to supply the family, of adding the improvements that finances will permit, and of bettering the appearance of the farmstead is gradually changing the outlook for the cotton farm family.

Outside Relations

The neighborhood church and consolidated school are the only organizations which serve the family in a social and educational way. The school district covers from sixty to two hundred square miles. Within it there are a half dozen or more churches of four or five Protestant denominations and one or two villages and probably one large town. Community clubs were organized after the consolidation program and many of the people attended monthly meetings at the schoolhouse. In a few cases the discarded schoolhouse was saved for a community center and clubs were organized on a large neighborhood basis. The large community club served a reasonable number of people while automobiles were plentiful, but now the attendance at these gatherings is limited almost to the people in the town or section of the district where the school is located. People who live at a distance attend school events occasionally when their children are on a public program.

The church is now the only organization which regularly serves the family. The interest in church work decreased during the prosperous years and some people have not returned to it. Most of the leadership must come from the superior families in the communities or those with better educational and financial opportunities than the average. The summer revival meetings are important social occasions. The older people get emotional satisfaction out of the sermons on approved recreation for the young people when the minister condemns their innocent pleasures. The young people attend the meetings and join in the singing but are not disturbed by the condemnation of swimming, automobile riding, or card-playing. The minister may have in his series one sermon which makes suggestions for a desirable pattern of family life. This may cause a temporary improvement in the family relations which he declares sinful.

The man goes to the village or town and joins his neighbors in gossiping and whittling almost every Saturday afternoon. Many public questions are outlined and discussed by such gatherings. The man goes to the county seat once or twice during a session of court to see his friends from other parts of the county.

The woman spends most of her time at home. She calls on relatives in the community or neighbors on Sunday afternoon, usually accompanied by her husband and the small children. When she goes shopping she takes the young children and stays all day. This trip is a real social event for her because she often sees friends from other communities whom she has not seen since her shopping trip several weeks or months before. She seldom attends a meeting which is planned for women either in church or the home demonstration organization. She thinks she is too busy to take the time away from home.

The young people must make their own recreation or find it at commercial amusement places like the movies and soda fountain. Very little is done at home to entertain them. When a home social is given it is usually unorganized and a general invitation is extended which brings people who cannot fit into the crowd without making unpleasant scenes. This is especially true when the rowdy boys get too much liquor before going to an affair where liquor has no place. If the family has friends or relatives in town, they are regarded as superior to the farm family, regardless of their social or financial position. The girl is always proud to date a boy from town though he may be inferior to her country friends. The boys from ten to fifteen years old congregate on Sunday afternoon at one of the homes or at a public place and play baseball or go to a swimming place. The young children have little chance to play with friends of their own age except when the mother visits where there are children or has a guest who brings them.

The family has daily mail delivery on the rural route. The county weekly paper and one farm magazine are about the only regular pieces of mail which the family gets. The older boys and girls correspond with their friends of the opposite sex and the woman writes to her sisters or other relatives who live in distant communities. The woman writes business letters for her husband if he has any.

There are three distinct social classes in the community. They are the more prosperous farmers and any professional people who may reside there; the small landowners and better class tenants; and those who are socially unaccepted because of illegitimacy in the family, immoral practices of one member, or failure to make enough money to live up to the standards of the community without aid from a charitable institution or individual donations. Financial gain, a worthwhile accomplishment, or educational improvement raises a family socially, while departure from accepted moral standards by one member of the family may place the others in the unaccepted class.

ROUTINE OF LIVING

The man is the proud holder of the place of authority in the cotton farm family. He regards his opinion and judgment as the best in the family on any question that arises. He handles the finances and transacts all business deals, directs the field work, and passes on the social and recreational activities which the children take part in. The woman accepts the dictation of the man without resentment though she often sees him use poor judgment. The children accept his orders but find a way to work out their own plan of living without his knowing when they disobey him.

The woman keeps the clothes clean and mended and serves three meals a day the year around. In addition she voluntarily works in the field four or five hours each afternoon during the crop season.

Both boys and girls work as day laborers, without pay, in the crop from the age of ten or eleven till the boy is twenty-one and the girl is married or at work in town. The children attend school during school hours and help with the work when they return home.

The financial status of the family is indefinite as was stated before. The children do not know how much it costs to maintain a home or to clothe them and the woman has no idea of the cost of groceries which are bought for a year. If credit lasts till harvest time there is little concern about the financial standing. The woman has a tendency to be economical and the man may be stingy with his family but free with his neighbors. The children feel that they do not get their share of the family money and they realize that the father is not a good manager.

The man gets out of bed about daybreak each morning, makes the fires, and calls all members of the household. The woman goes immediately to the kitchen and prepares the breakfast of hot biscuits, with butter and syrup or fried meat and gravy. The girls may set the table and put the house in order before breakfast. The man and boys feed the livestock and chop enough wood to cook dinner with. The members of the family hurriedly eat breakfast and leave one at a time for work or school. The small children frequently try to follow the others away and must be chased after and brought back by the mother.

After breakfast the woman milks the cow, feeds the chickens, makes the butter, and gathers the vegetables for dinner and supper. The daughter will help her as she is directed. She prepares enough of one or two kinds of vegetables for the two meals and cooks them together. The family does not object to cold or warmed-over food. Usually all members eat dinner together in the middle of the day when school is not in session. After dinner the man and boys sit on the porch. The woman will sit or lie down and rest while the girls wash the dishes. Then everybody goes to the field for the afternoon. The young children play at the end of the row where the mother hoes or picks cotton. About an hour before sundown the woman and small children go to the house to milk the cow, collect the eggs, and put supper on the table. When the other members of the family come in they eat and go to bed.

All field work is discontinued from Saturday at noon till Monday morning. On Saturday afternoons the man and boys go to town while the woman and girls iron, patch, clean yards, and put the house in order for Sunday. If the girl feels bad she is excused from the field but must do most of the housework during the time she is out so the mother can work longer hours. The woman wants to work in the field because she has always been accustomed to it. Even if the man wants her to spend her time at the house she is inclined to find an excuse to go. It may be that she feels better outside when in reality she dislikes housework, or it may be that she wants to lead the children in the phase of work they are assigned to do. The girls dislike field work and are embarrassed to have their more fortunate acquaintances who do not have to do this type of work see them in the field. Field work has a tendency to depress them and give them a feeling of inferiority.

The father is intolerant of his daughter's early suitors. He does not think she should waste her time with boys. She is the victim of many emotional upsettings as an outgrowth of family clashes in her early courting days. However, the father eventually calms down and accepts the boy friends. The mother is as a rule sympathetic with the girl but must takes sides with the man. The boys are generally free to work out their own plans for recreation and social life without the dictation of the father at an earlier age than the girls.

When the boys reach the age of fifteen or sixteen they get a small amount of the money as the father has cash on hand and sometimes a new suit in the fall. They leave school at fourteen or fifteen years of age before completing the grammar grades. They must stay at home for a few days each spring to work even at an earlier age. After a boy fails to make his grade because of absence he does not care to return. The parents have the attitude that they made a living with little education beyond the third or fourth grade and that children likewise need no more. The boys do not as a rule care to continue their studies.

If a boy belongs to a 4-H club, he has a hard time following the instructions of the extension agent. The man thinks his farming methods are the best and he blames crop failures on the weather or insects. If a boy slips in a scientific method which proves profitable, the father is quick to adopt it and claim it as his own idea. The boy gets some inspiration and social contacts from a 4-H club if he is willing to continue it after leaving school.

The mother is no more willing to accept the new ideas which the daughter brings home from the 4-H club or the home economics class than the father is those of the boy. However, she will not openly announce to the community that she rejects them.

The boy is not neat or orderly in the house. He expects the entire family to keep track of his personal belongings, such as razor, shaving cream, pocket knife, and wearing apparel. He likes to hunt and fish. He has a gun and one or two dogs after leaving school. He often goes hunting with his father or neighborhood boys and brings home squirrels, quail, rabbits, or other game suitable for food.

There is little real companionship, however, between the father and his sons. Corporal punishment was the method of disciplining them when they were small and the children developed an attitude of fear. They resent dictation at an early age and do not hesitate to refer to the father as "the old man" when talking to other boys or to grown people.

The members of the family appear fairly well-groomed when they are dressed for special occasions. The man and boys do not shave daily unless they are going to a social affair. Sometimes the man will let his beard grow all the week. Bathing facilities are inconvenient, so the Saturday night bath is about the only provision for cleanliness unless one is to dress for a special event. However, faces and hands are washed several times a day. The men wash their faces before each meal.

The man ridicules formality and the boys tease the girls if they attempt to observe everyday courtesies and good table manners in the family. This lack of training and practice in social customs is a great handicap to the children when they are grown. Even before they are grown it gives them a feeling of inferiority at school and in social groups.

The family discipline is tyrannical, but the children soon find a way to do many things they want to without the knowledge of the parents. The parents preach to them about doing right and being a credit to themselves and to the family. There is a high regard for respectable moral standards in the family and the parents are eager to have their children uphold them.

The Out-of-School Girl

The cotton farm girl left school in the first or second year of high school after having been absent too much to pass her year's work. She had to stay at home and help with the housework when her mother was sick or for other reasons which could have been avoided. The parents reminded the daughter that she should help them to repay for the services she received when a child. She was unwilling to miss time from her classes at first but finally did it without complaining. After failing in some subjects she preferred to stay at home rather than join a class of younger girls in repeating the work.

The girl realized that she would be lonely and that she would long to see her classmates and friends. She saw nothing in the future but hard labor at the house and in the field. If she has brothers near her age, they will take her to the social gatherings in the community and to the young people's church meetings. If there are no brothers she may be able to form a friendship with a young man who will take her to the places she wishes to go. Otherwise she will soon lose contact with the young crowd and be left alone. The school girls of a community clique together and regard those a year or two older or those out-of-school as outsiders. There are usually not enough of the latter class to form a separate crowd or clique. The girl takes little active part in church and Sunday-School work in spite of the fact that she has a great deal of time. Nothing is done to get her started in these activities and she does not push herself forward.

She works as a household servant and field laborer without pay. She has no money of her own and must ask for the money for clothes and other necessities. The mother realizes that she needs better clothes than the average for the family so she makes every effort to get them. She often sells chickens and eggs to provide the daughter with a new dress for a special occasion. The daughter visits friends and relatives in other communities. She usually picks revival meeting week as the visiting time. There she meets the young people.

The girl has little opportunity to read if she likes reading and can find any interesting books or magazines. The mother thinks reading a waste of time and constantly reminds the daughter of household duties or her own clothes which are being neglected while she is reading. It is hard for the girl to find time to write letters in spite of the fact that she has little responsibility or definitely outlined work to do when she is not working in the field. She has little opportunity to manage the house unless the mother is sick. Then she likely has instructions for the menus and other things from the bed. If the girl had training in home economics or club work while in school she will likely forget most of it before starting a home of her own.

If the girl had enough training to make her conscious of the lack of culture and refinement and the family refuses to coöperate with her in trying to raise these standards, she will likely have many unhappy moments and disappointments which will end in her abandoning the idea and drifting back to the old habits.

The girl would like to have a career but she knows there is no possibility of her entering the business world. She looks upon marriage as the one way to change her station in life. She envies the girls who can go out and make their own living and does not consider homemaking a business or profession. She will likely marry a boy in the same parish if not in the immediate community. She will probably be married at the parsonage or courthouse and the event will receive little notice or comment by people other than the families who will approve or object to the match. The boy is likely as self-satisfied as his father and sees no need of formality and ceremony in the home. He may ridicule the girl who wants him to observe the common courtesies of a refined home if any of these ideals remain with her after the disappointment experienced when she attempted to change the practices of her brothers and sisters. The girl may struggle along for a while and then copy the home she grew up in unless she has somebody to encourage her and unless she can change the attitude of her husband.

CHAPTER VI

THE TOBACCO FARM FAMILY

THE TOBACCO farm family of eastern North Carolina owns a farm consisting of about twenty acres of land. Six or seven acres are planted in tobacco and the rest is used for growing corn, truck, and other crops in a diversified farm program. The tobacco is planted in February and marketed in September or October. There are six or seven children in the family. All members of the family help with the crop as soon as they are old enough. The man hauls the tobacco to market in his touring car or truck, if he owns one; otherwise he hires it hauled. He receives a check for each load but he must use a large part of it to pay debts for fertilizer and living expenses incurred while the crop was being produced.

PHYSICAL SURROUNDINGS

The house is located on the highest place on the farm. A half dozen or more houses may be built on the small hill or elevation with the farms extending out in various directions. The house is painted on the outside, and the inside is finished with plaster which is in need of repair. The floors are unfinished and bare. There are usually six rooms in the house. Three are used for bedrooms and the others for living room, dining room, and kitchen. The house has screens in the doors and in some of the windows.

There is a general lack of organization and order in arrangement and storage of household equipment and personal articles. Wearing apparel and toilet articles belonging to one member of the family may be found anywhere in the house except in the owner's bedroom. Farm implements are kept in the house and often one bedroom is used to store tobacco in from the time it is taken from the curing barn till it is graded and taken to market.

The water supply is from a surface pump in the yard or on the front or back porch. Wood or kerosene is used for cooking fuel. Wood is used in a fireplace or stove for heating the house. There is no solid foundation under the house, the wind penetrates through the cracks in the floors, and heating the rooms to a comfortable temperature is difficult.

The furniture is plain and reasonably substantial. Some of it has been in the family for a long time though few pieces have real value as antiques. There is a Victrola and often an organ in the living room. The china is cheap and breaks easily. The knives and forks have wooden handles and wear only two or three years. Few articles of this kind are nice enough to become heirlooms.

The yard has several shade trees. There is no grass or sod. There are several flower beds in the yard. They are bordered with snuff bottles, car tires, cart wheels, and rocks. The yard is swept clean every few days with a yard broom. The farm buildings look unsightly as they are scattered all around the yard. A wire fence separates the yard from the barnyard and pastures.

There is, however, a great deal of pride and interest in the home. It is kept clean but in a poor state of repair. Since the woman works in the field a part of the year and must do her housework without modern conveniences, she can give only a minimum amount of time to cultivating flowers and caring for the yard.

The Food Supply

The family has far less home-grown food than is necessary for a year-round balanced diet. Vegetables are grown in the spring and fall and a few are stored for winter. A small flock of chickens is kept for meat and eggs. One or two hogs are butchered each year. Most of the feed for the livestock is grown on the farm. However, in the rush of the tobacco harvest the food and feed supply may be forgotten. Sometimes the garden is left to grow up in weeds, and the cow is put in the pasture with the calf. Naturally, this neglect proves expensive if the tobacco brings a good price and it is detrimental if the price is too low to leave surplus cash after expenses are paid.

Outside Relations

The family lives in a neighborhood composed of from five to sixty or more families. This neighborhood is a part of a community built up around one or more villages. The area of the community is about fourteen square miles and the population ranges from 300 to 1,000 white people. The consolidated school which the children attend is usually located in the largest village. This village is the community center. There are several country stores in the various neighborhoods. They supply staple groceries and serve as a gathering place for the men. Rural mail routes reach most of the neighborhoods.

There are seven or eight churches representing various branches of the four Protestant denominations in the community. The churches have conflicting creeds and standards regarding approved recreation. If the man and woman were reared in the same denomination, the family will belong to one church. Otherwise the man and woman hold on to their own denomination but attend services at both churches. The children select between the two and usually join one or the other at an early age.

The children attend Sunday-School every Sunday and the parents go with them on "Preaching Day" once or twice a month. Services always begin late, so the men who arrive on time stand around the front door and visit till the singing starts. The women congregate inside and talk till the organ sounds and the services are opened. Everybody lingers and talks after the benediction.

The minister and his wife accompany the family home for dinner once or twice a year. In the summer revival services are held for a week or more. This is a big social occasion. The visiting minister frequently lays down rules which are too strict for the existing customs in the community. If the parents attempt to get the children to give up movies, cards, and Sunday swims because the minister condemned them, numerous family clashes arise. The gossipers justify their criticisms of the young people by the minister's statements regarding their conduct. Such services often make the young people skeptical and critical of their denomination.

The family belongs to one of the two approved social classes. They are the natives, and the people who have moved into the county within the past fifty years. The casual observer may not recognize these classes, but after staying for a while a visitor finds the feeling of distinction quite noticeable. The people who trace their ancestry to the pre-Revolutionary days resent any "outsider's" attempting to take the lead in public affairs. This is especially true of the women. The classes mix and sometimes intermarry, though many comments are passed on such an occurrence.

Two or more families may exchange work during the tobacco harvest. The women visit while they string tobacco, and the men chat or exchange ideas as they meet at the barn while hauling the tobacco leaves from the near-by fields. A great deal of visiting is done in the community, usually on Sunday afternoon. If a family is to spend the day with relatives or friends, arrangements are made in advance.

The woman has little leisure time and few contacts outside of the immediate neighborhood. The girls have a great many social contacts while they are in school but the number decreases rapidly as the months lapse after they leave school. The woman goes to the county seat or to another town three or four times a year to buy clothes for the family.

The man and boys have a reasonable amount of leisure time and spend it with friends in the community and other parts of the county. The young boys belong to a crowd which enjoys fishing, swimming, and baseball as main sports. The older boys join the father and other men at the so called "spit and whittle" clubs at the country store. There the men chew tobacco and whittle up all the pine strips from packing boxes they can find. They discuss current issues and complain about the weather.

An important occasion for the men is an informal gathering of the men from the entire county at the courthouse on first Monday which is the meeting date for the county boards of various kinds. Criminal court week is just as important for the men. On these days the courthouse square and adjoining vacant lots compose a busy section of the town. Patent medicine agents and various other peddlers begin business early in the morning, church organizations sell lunch, and the sheriff sells property which has been seized for taxes. The men gather in small groups around the building and in the halls to discuss pending legislation and personal affairs. The men keep reasonably well informed on public issues through contacts with other men from various parts of the county on court days. The women seldom go to the county seat on these occasions since they are regarded as social and business gatherings of men.

The woman probably had two or three years more of schooling than the man she married, but his broad contacts in comparison with the few which she had outside of the home soon raised his educational level to that of hers. The couple grew up in the same community and bought or inherited property near their birthplaces. They will likely live their entire lives in the community.

Routine of Living

The family is paternal. The man handles the money, directs the work, play, and religious life of the family. The wife and children ask for money and get it if he thinks they need the amount they ask for. The oldest boy will probably have a small share of the crop to sell for his money. The man buys the groceries an article at a time as he goes to the store. He also buys his clothes, farm supplies, and tobacco. The woman and children try to provide for his physical comforts when he is at the house. He demands his meals on time and food that suits his appetite. He wants it on the table as soon as he comes in from work. After the meal he sits on the porch or in the living room and smokes his pipe or reads the paper or a farm magazine till time to return to the field or to go to bed. Between crop seasons he hunts, fishes, or joins his neighbors at the neighborhood store to discuss local happenings, high taxes, and hard times. He thinks that the man should do none of the housework or even the milking. This fact is illustrated by a conversation between a typical farmer and a county office seeker. The politician called late one afternoon and after a brief chat remarked that he had to go home since it was about milking time. The farmer looked puzzled and asked if the wife was sick or away from home. In spite of the attitude indicated by this anecdote, the man rises first in the morning, makes the fires, then calls the other members of the family.

The woman does the housework with the help of the girls, cares for the children, feeds the chickens, milks and feeds the cow, hoes the garden, and helps with the field work. She begins the day at daybreak during the summer and at about five-thirty in the morning during the winter months. Her work day ends at about eight o'clock at night and she has little rest between the beginning and the end. She cooks a heavy breakfast and serves it as the members of the family come in singly. She seldom sits down with any of them to eat this meal. In summer she milks the cow while the girls wash the dishes, then they join the man and boys in the field. They assist with all work except the plowing. At about nine-thirty the woman goes to the house to gather vegetables and to cook dinner and supper. She usually brings in wood and water necessary for preparing the meal. The family eats dinner as a group except in the busiest crop season. The woman leaves the table several times during the meal for food and serving dishes. She cooks a variety of vegetables at each meal to try to suit the varied appetites of the different members of the family. This necessarily requires extra work. After dinner she and the girls wash the dishes and join the men when they are ready to return to the field. About one and one-half hours are taken from work at noon. The woman works till almost sunset, then goes to the house to do the night work. Supper is put on the table as it was left at dinnertime and the members of the family eat as they are ready. The girls put the kitchen in order while the woman gets the young children ready for bed. The woman and one girl stay at the house one morning during the week and Saturday to wash and to clean house. They do the sewing and mending on rainy days and when the field work is finished. The woman's rôle in the family is mainly to provide physical comforts. She is usually tired, irritable and ready to nag at the husband and the children when anythings goes wrong.

The children are farm laborers. Both boys and girls begin work in the field at the age of seven or eight. The baby goes to the field and plays or stays at the house in care one of the young children. The children work for long hours and are scolded or punished for neglect of duty. Saturday afternoon is the only leisure time they have during the crop season. They go to school regularly until they are fourteen years of age. Then the boys begin to stop because of indifference, or at the request of the father who wants their labor as it is needed. The school bus route is long, so the children must leave home early in the morning and return late in the afternoon. Often they rush off in the morning without eating breakfast and with a part of the food cooked for breakfast wrapped in paper to eat at noon. They see their parents very little on school days.

If the boy decides to finish high school he may want to attend an agricultural college. The father opposes this desire and says it is useless to spend money to teach a boy to be a farmer. Usually the boy is forced to abandon the idea of going to college and has to work as a farm laborer till he is about eighteen. Then the father gives him a share in the crop. The boy spends his money freely and has a rather leisurely life between crop seasons till he gets married. Then he starts to farm alone on rented land or a part of his father's farm if there is any untilled land which he can clear. The boy is not interested in farming but knows nothing else to do.

The rôle of the girls in the family is generally that of unpaid servants. They have litle part in managing the home. The mother does not have the time and patience to teach them to go ahead on their own initiative with the cooking and sewing. The 4-H club girls and home economics students find it difficult to carry out their practice assignments because they do not have freedom in the kitchen.

The oldest girl had her first boy friend at the age of fifteen or sixteen. This caused a family clash because the parents did not want her to have dates. She slipped around with her dates for a while, then gained the sympathy of her mother. The father has little confidence in men so he does not want to trust his daughter in their company. The parents are more sensible about the courtships of the other daughters than they are of the oldest one. If the girl wants to train for a business or professional career, the parents say it is useless for her to get an education because she will soon marry.

The family seldom sits down for a social visit unless there is a guest. When any of the members read, they do it individually. If they have a musical instrument they may listen to the music in a group. Little attention is paid to the observance of everyday courtesies in the family circle. The woman thinks little of teaching the children good table manners or other social customs in the home. Lack of knowledge of these rules has a tendency to make the children self-conscious when they are among strangers or people with whom they wish to stand well. The mother is also too busy to pay much attention to her personal appearance. However, when she dresses for special occasions she can make a good appearance.

The children get an idea of a broader life in school and often become dissatisfied with the home and family life. They may resent the dictation of the family minister regarding forbidden recreation, and revolt at the rules of behavior that their parents lay down regarding where they go and when they must return. These little misunderstandings may lead to frequent clashes between the parents and children and cause them to lose confidence in each other.

The very nature of tobacco culture with its long growing season, detailed labor requiring many workers, short harvesting period, long hours both day and night for curing, storing, grading by the women, and long trips which the man must make to market the crop, disrupts family life. The fact that the woman and girls devote a great deal of time to the labor on the farm keeps the family from being as well managed as it might be with a different division of labor.

The Out-of-School Girl

The girl in the tobacco farm family left school at fifteen or sixteen years of age when she had started her first year in high-school. Either she found her home duties too heavy to allow her to study enough to pass her work or she just got tired of going. She works for long hours in the field and at the house but has little incentive to do her best.

She does not like the interior of the house but her mother will not permit her to change it. Out-of-date calendars on the walls, framed certificates which have little meaning, and a great many family photographs annoy the girl. When she suggests making changes to bring the house up to date her mother resents the suggestions. If the girl cooks a meal she must get detailed instructions just before starting and carry them out. She is not privileged to plan the meal and follow her own recipes.

She has no money of her own and must ask her father for enough to buy the necessities as she needs them. The father often thinks she is unreasonable with her requests. Although she has more clothes than any other member of the family she has the habit of complaining about not having enough. She wants books or magazines and other things which the small amount of money she asks will not permit her to buy.

There are few girls in the community who are out of school, so this girl has a rather lonely life. She is soon dropped by the high school crowd when she discontinues her studies. Unless she has a suitor who takes her to social gatherings she is left out almost entirely. She goes to church and to a movie occasionally.

The parents do not approve of her courting and rather discourage her in bringing her boy friends home. They think the girl has a good home and that she is better off in it than married to any of the boys with whom she associates. The parents' attitude in this matter is to a great extent responsible for the lack of companionship which should exist between them and the daughter. The girl goes to her girl friends for consolation and advice rather than to her mother. However, the relation between the mother and daughter is much friendlier than that between the girl and her father.

The girl may be unable to accept the narrow religious creed of the parents. If so, she will be a constant source of worry to the parents who think more of her soul than her chance of happiness either as a girl or a woman.

The girl will eventually become engaged to one of the boys in the community and plan a quiet home wedding with the help of the parents who objected to her marrying. The mother will point out the many hardships of married life and urge the girl to stay at home. However, the girl goes on with the plans which the parents feel it their duty to coöperate in. The boy has two or three years less schooling than the girl. His vision of a family is the same as that of his father; so he naturally expects the girl to take her place in the field as his mother did.

The girl will enter married life after two or three years of unrewarded toil. Likely, she has formed the habit of being dissatisfied with herself and everything she has. Most of her home economics training has been cast aside if she had any and she can do nothing but copy the home she grew up in.

The girl wanted a business career and accepts marriage as a poor substitute. The boy farms because he can do nothing else. The couple will talk about the careers they might have had and think of the farm as a place where they landed because careers were closed to them, and it will be hard for either to put his best into making a success of farming or of farm home-making.

CHAPTER VII

THE FISHING COMMUNITY FAMILY

THE FISHING community of the Chesapeake Bay section of Virginia covers an area of about 500 acres of land. The average population is 1,400 but it varies from less than 100 to more than 3,000. The village may be located on an island which can be reached only by boat, on an island connected with the mainland by a causeway, or on the waterfront of the mainland. The families of isolated islands have individualities which are not mentioned in the description of the typical family. The community has a school, one or more churches, a post office, and several general stores. One or more physicians live either in the community itself, or near enough to practice there.

THE HOUSE

The family lives in a house built in the general style of architecture which is used in the community. This house is a tall compact two-story frame building without porches. The design of the houses is sometimes referred to as "ship builder's architecture" since the house resembles a ship in height and width. Early carpenters who built ships planned and built the residences. The carpenter is still the recognized authority on house planning in the community. Often a woman has a new idea for convenience which she wants used in the house which is being built or remodeled but finds it difficult to get the carpenter to use it. He will tell her of other houses which he has built in a certain way and how well the owners like them in order to try to get the privilege of carrying out his own ideas. The man usually thinks the carpenter knows best and the woman abandons her ideas and spends years regretting that the work was not done in a different way.

The house has five or six rooms. Two large ones on the front with one or two small ones forming an L at the back make the first floor. There are two upstairs rooms over the front ones. The first floor front rooms are used for a living room and a bedroom. The ones behind are the dining room and kitchen. Those upstairs are bedrooms. The living room and one bedroom are heated with wood or coal stoves. Wood or kerosene is used for cooking fuel. When the man can arrange for wood to be brought to his home by boat from a distant shore it is fairly cheap, but all fuel delivered by truck is quite expensive. All rooms are wired for electric drop lights from the ceiling in the center of the room. The walls are papered and the floors are stained with varnish. Some rugs are used. The furniture is sturdy and comfortable but the house is over furnished. Color combinations are not carefully made and vivid colors are used.

The lawn is grassed and generally kept mowed. The front yard is free from rubbish, but tin cans and other discarded materials are noticeable in the back yard. The pump and clothesline are in the side or back yard. There is no fence or enclosure around the yard.

The family owns the house and will pass it on to the coming generation. There is a great deal of pride in the ownership of a house and lot. Parents feel that they should leave some property to their children and they work to make this possible. Old people have been known to ask for charity rather than mortgage the land which they expect to leave to the children.

INCOME AND FOOD SUPPLY

The man earns practically all the cash which the family has. The older boys may help with light work on the water and contribute their earnings to the family purse. When the boy is sixteen or seventeen years of age he goes to the water with his father. The man works for weekly wages or for a per cent of the sales of sea foods gathered by the boat crew with which he works. The man may own a share in a boat but the average fisherman does not own a boat. The income is indefinite and varies with the seasons. There is no income during December, January, and February, unless the man works with an oystering crew. The people who depend on the oyster and clam business have little income during the summer months. However, the wise fisherman will diversify his fishing if possible. Like the worker in any other industry, he is dependent on the demand for the product for obtaining work out of his special line.

There is not much variety in the diet. Sea foods are used extensively on the family table. They may be taken from the market supply or caught near the home by the women and children. Several bushels of fish are salted for use during the winter months. October is the month for curing the fish. Little milk is used in the daily diet. Lack of pasture land and space to grow feed together with the sanitary arrangements in the community make it impractical to produce milk in quantity in the community. Some canned milk is used and dairies have milk routes to various homes. Fruits and vegetables are scarce. The gardens are small and usually provide only a few spring vegetables. Figs grow in large quantities but they are the only fruit of any importance in the back yards.

Making a living is easy for the fishing community family when nature and the market are favorable, but when these fail there are no other resources to turn to. The family has comforts and luxuries during normal times but puts little aside for rainy days. A bad season means lowered living standards and sometimes the necessity of outside relief.

Outside Relations

The family has a great many contacts with the neighbors and a limited number with people from distant communities or cities. The men gather at the various stores after work hours to chat, eat cookies or candy and drink soft drinks. If they want stronger drinks they go on the boats or to specified places for them. The man goes to church regularly and to a movie occasionally.

The women gather in various homes for informal chats almost daily. This is as popular a pastime for them as the store gathering is for the men. The wife goes to church two or three times a month and to the school league when her children are on the program. When the woman is sick the neighbors nurse her and care for her family till she is well. The woman goes to a large town once or twice a year to buy clothes and other household needs which are not supplied by the local stores. The oldest girl takes this responsibility when she is about sixteen.

Usually the leaders among the women are teachers who married and became citizens of the community. These women and city women who visit in the community do a great deal to direct the thinking and household practices of the community women. A guest may teach her hostess a new recipe or a food principle and all the community will adopt it within a few weeks. Likewise these visitors bring in new ideas on child training, clothes, and home management. Occasionally the woman will make a trip to the city on the boat which takes fish to market. Likewise the city friends and relatives make the trip to the community.

The children have their friends and see them frequently. The small boys assemble on vacant lots or in an alley to play marbles, or other games. The small girls play dolls and dressing up in grown-up clothes. The young people visit, attend dances, movies, parties, and other social gatherings. Practically all the young people and children swim every day during the summer.

Routine of Living

The household schedule must be made and adjusted to fit the working hours of the man. It varies with the seasons and the kinds of fishing he does. If he does pound fishing he leaves home at about three o'clock in the morning and returns from ten to twelve hours later. Another type of fishing may make it necessary for him to go to sea for two or three weeks at a time. During the winter he may be at home for two or three months mending nets and overhauling the boat which he works on.

When school is in session the woman must serve meals several times a day in order to fit them into the leisure hours of all members of the family. She gets up about an hour before the man leaves for work to fix breakfast and pack his lunch. She will go back to bed and stay till about an hour before the children leave for school and fix another breakfast and several lunches if any children go on a bus to high school. She has a little free time before preparing the twelve-o'clock lunch for the children who go to the local school. The next meal is served when the man returns from work and the high school children get home. If the man is at sea the dinner is served when the children return from school just the same. All members of the family usually eat the evening meal together after the man or woman returns thanks. The woman prepares sandwiches for herself and the children to eat before retiring at about nine o'clock. The well-being of the children gets first consideration if there is any difference or preference to be shown between them and the husband.

When the man is at sea he eats with the crew on the boat. Each man may take some food or one may buy the groceries and charge for the meals of the members of the fishing crew. Most men who work on the water are fair cooks, and they can take turns preparing the meals if necessary.

The woman does the housework and laundry with some help from the girls. The boys keep the lawn, make fires, and work the garden with the mother's help. The children below school age run errands for the mother. They take a note to the storekeeper and bring home small items of groceries. It is not unusual for the child to forget about the errand and stop to play with one or two young friends who were sent to the store to make purchases for their mothers.

The woman makes most of the purchases and the man pays the bills when he gets his weekly or seasonal pay. She knows little of the cost of operating the house so long as there is credit. She always has money in her purse and she gives some to the children for candy and soft drinks almost daily. The mother has no idea of the amount she spends or gives the children during a week or month.

The young people read or play a mechanical musical instrument in the early evening either alone or with neighbors who come in. Occasionally all the members of the family spend an evening listening to the experiences the father relates about his recent trip to a distant port or at sea.

The members of the family are courteous to each other though harsh language may be used in case of anger. There is usually a common religious conviction and all members attend church together.

Since the man is away from home a great deal of the time and has irregular hours even when he is at home daily, most of the responsibility of organizing and directing family life falls on the woman. She must handle discipline problems which arise, care for the children when they are sick, settle their disputes, and train them in manners and customs. Her ideas of family life and culture play a larger part in shaping the ideals of the children than those of the father. She gives a great deal more of such training to the girls than to the boys since she has a closer association with them than she does with the boys after they are old enough to go to sea.

THE OUT-OF-SCHOOL GIRL

The daughter in the fishing family quit school in the first or second year of high school because she got tired of going. She was about fifteen years of age when she decided that a high-school diploma was not worth the years of work ahead of her. The girls have about three years more schooling than the boys, but the boys learn a trade or way of making a living immediately after dropping their studies.

The girl has a leisurely and carefree life after leaving school. The mother thinks she will have to assume the responsibilities of housework when she is married and thinks that she is favoring her by shielding her from this type of work as long as she can.

She has attractive clothes which are bought ready-made or made by her mother. They are kept in a good condition by the girl and her mother. The girl gets money for clothes and for recreation as she asks for it. She usually thinks she should have more but has no idea of the amount she gets weekly or monthly.

There are several idle girls in the community who form a friendship clique and spend a great deal of time together. They meet informally in various homes to talk, make candy, and exchange experiences of their recreational activities. The young people attend dances and movies in other communities. Enough boy friends of girls in the crowd have cars to provide a way for most couples to go to these entertainments. The girl must get home at a set hour or cause a family clash when she arrives at a later hour.

The girl is generally restless and wants to be going somewhere. She realizes that she is merely marking time and has no definite goal in sight other than to get married. Marriage is not generally admitted as her goal although it is her only plan for the future. After leaving school, she does little to improve herself mentally or socially. If she had home economics training in school she loses most of the knowledge and technique during her idle years.

The girl meets young men from other communities

and continues some of the friendships formed at school. She marries two or three years after leaving school. The mother wants her daughter to be popular with the young folks and the father has little opportunity to interfere with her courting even if he has the inclination to do so. However, little of the courting is done at home.

After she assumes the responsibilities of making a home, the girl must form a new philosophy of life as well as learn the technique of housekeeping. She is likely to begin her married life in the community she grew up in and have the help of her mother while she is adjusting herself to her husband, home, and community as a homemaker.

CHAPTER VIII

THE POTATO FARM FAMILY

The potato farm family of eastern Virginia lives in or near a village. A county in this section is made up from five to ten communities of about 100 square miles each. There are five or six villages or small towns in each community with farm houses built close together on the roads connecting them. The high school district is the only recognized community boundary. Social and business activities extend throughout the county to the extent that the county resembles a city with each village representing a residential and small business section. Each community has one or more grammar schools, a high school, banks, six or more post offices, several small general stores, a moving picture house, and seven or more Protestant churches. There is no one recognized community center.

Like the community, the county has no recognized business center. The county seat is a mere village with a courthouse. The county offices are scattered in the various villages. All villages are connected by a telephone system and good roads. Most of the villages have electricity from a central power plant.

Practically all the people were born and reared in the county. Many of the homesteads have never had a deed, since they are held by descendants of the original settlers who received grants from the King of England.

Physical Surroundings

The house in the potato farm community is a story and a half dormer window colonial type, or a compact two-story A-roof type. It is said that in colonial times a man's social standing was determined by the number of rooms in his house and taxes were twice as much on a two-story building as the one-story. Therefore, the story and a half structure was used to decrease taxes as rooms were increased.

In the dormer type house at least three rooms face the road on the ground floor. There is a large room with one or two rooms above it, then a small room connected by a low roof with another section about two-thirds as high as the large one. These sections were called "big room, colonade, and kitchen." The house has six or seven rooms of different floor levels. This house seldom has a central heating plant.

If the house was built within the past fifty years it is a two-story A-roof type with eight or more rooms and a front porch. This may have a windmill pump for the water system in the house and a central heating system or several stoves. In either style of architecture the house is painted white or light tan.

The walls are plastered and the old pine floors are painted or stained. The furniture is antique or a substantial modern type. The family has a few pieces which were handed down from the early settlers and others which have been added by other generations. There is a supply of linen, china, and silver for everyday use and other for special occasions. Some of this was inherited and other accumulated over a period of years.

The house has a living room, dining room, kitchen with space for a dining table, and a bedroom for each two members of the family at least. The dining room is used for the family living room and meals are served in the kitchen except when guests are present. The kitchen is large and inconvenient, though in general the house is reasonably well organized with provision for privacy, work, and social life. Storage facilities are often inadequate and time is lost in searching for lost articles.

The lawn is grassed and has a few shade trees and old shrubs. Summer flowers are sometimes used for borders. There is little foundation shrubbery or other evergreens in the yard. The house has an open foundation or one with a lath inclosure. The very old houses are built close to the ground so that an inclosed foundation makes little difference in the appearance. The windmill and farm buildings are grouped toward the back of the house. The farmstead has a substantial and orderly appearance. The family has a pride in the home and each member is willing to help keep it in a good state of repair and attractive in appearance.

INCOME AND FOOD SUPPLY

The farmer, with the help of hired labor and a little from his sons between school terms, together with seasonal help from other members of the family, cultivates about thirty acres of land. White potatoes and sweet potatoes constitute the principal crops. Some small truck and a little feed are grown. The white potatoes are planted in February or March and harvested in June or July. Sweet potatoes are planted in covered beds in March or April and transplanted in the fields in May. They are marketed from late August through October.

All members of the family help cut the potatoes for planting. This requires about a week of intensive work the last of February. The harvest season lasts about three weeks. Negroes from the city come to the farm and pick up potatoes for a set price per barrel. All members of the family help in some way with the harvest though the woman and girls seldom pick up potatoes. Beside the market crop, a spring garden provides some vegetables to be eaten fresh and a few for canning. Late summer vegetables are grown for canning. A small flock of chickens and one or two hogs are kept.

It has been the custom to operate both the farm and the home on a credit basis and pay the bills from the white potato crop but this practice is changing. More interest is shown in home-grown foods and cash payments for household expenses. The family usually has enough money or credit to maintain a standard of living as high as that of the average family living on a salary in the city. The home, food, clothes, car, and recreation or advancement compare favorably with those of the middle class city family.

Outside Relations

The potato farm family has a great many social contacts with relatives and friends through home visiting as well as with people from other communities in church and business organizations. Family gatherings are held on holidays, anniversaries, and birthdays. Once or twice a year parents entertain their grown children and families. Each daughter in turn invites the relatives on her side of the family for a dinner. On another day she invites the husband's relatives to dinner. The season between Thanksgiving and Christmas, as well as the holidays, is a popular time for family entertainment. Married children visit their parents and meet their brothers and sisters on Sunday afternoons throughout the year. The family goes to a seashore resort for a picnic occasionally, to church regularly, to school entertainments, and to the annual county fair.

The man meets his friends at the local store. This is a social center for the farmers. The minister, doctor, and business men occasionally join the crowd. In some stores chairs or benches are provided for these visitors around the stove in winter and at the entrance in summer. Here current topics are discussed and the storekeeper to a great extent directs the trend of thought of the crowd on the various issues. The man goes to the county seat on business occasionally. He attends farmers' meetings in the community and at the county seat.

The woman belongs to one or more organizations in her church. She attends local meetings monthly and county or district ones three or four times a year. She does her shopping in one of the larger villages or towns once or twice a month. She goes to a movie occasionally and to the school league meetings when her children are on the program.

The young people have a great deal of social life with young people in their crowd and with those of other communities. On an average the girls belong to two organizations of a social nature and the boys to one. They dance, play cards, swim, visit, and go to movies. The young children visit with their mother and play with neighboring children. They swim, attend Sunday-School picnics, and go to movies.

The members of the potato farm family have poise and knowledge of social customs which make them at home in any group. There is no distinction between the people who live in the villages and those on the farms. Social classification is made by birth or manner of living.

ROUTINE OF LIVING

There are about five children in the family. The family is democratic in organization and government. The man and woman work coöperatively in rearing the children and planning the use of the family money. There is a fair division of labor, so that all members help with the work and everyone has his share of leisure time.

The man rises in the morning and lights the fires. The woman prepares breakfast while the man and boys milk the cows and feed the livestock. The oldest girl assists the children in getting ready for school and sets the table for breakfast. Then the woman washes the dishes, cares for the milk and prepares the vegetables for lunch and dinner. Before dinner she has some time for weekly jobs, such as getting the laundry ready for the washwoman, sewing, mending, and canning. She serves the midday meal at twelve o'clock. It is lunch while school is in session and dinner during the summer. The girl usually puts the house in order while the mother does the kitchen work. All members of the family sit down to the table together and the father offers a prayer of thanks. After lunch the man and boys read the paper or play the radio for a few minutes before returning to work. Except in the very busy season when the woman and girls help as time keepers or other workers in the crop, they rest for a few minutes after dinner is finished, then dress for the afternoon either to go away or to stay at home. Usually the men dress before eating the evening meal.

In the early evening the family assembles in the everyday living room to talk, read, or listen to a radio program. Each member of the family enters into the conversation just as each has some kind of duty in operating the home.

The man manages the business side of the farm but the woman usually knows the financial status and has her share of the surplus cash after bills are paid. She usually has money in her purse or the privilege of writing checks if there is a bank account. The children usually have spending money. The boys get pay for field work at home or they work for other people. The girls ask for their money as they need it and keep no account of the amount they get. The children feel that they get their share of the money and the parents often accuse them of spending it unwisely.

The family is usually well-groomed. The clothes are kept in good condition. Storage facilities are not always adequate; so time and energy are often lost in searching for personal articles when they are misplaced. The mother finds it hard to get the various members of the family to keep things in their right places after she points out such places.

The members of the family are courteous to each other. The parents are not tyrannical with the children but command their respect. Conflicts arise and must be settled by the parents, but due consideration is given to the children involved. The man and the woman usually agree on a set of rules for the children and coöperate in carrying them out. Corporal punishment is used some with the small children. The parents often find it necessary to reprimand the older boys and girls for teasing the younger children either while they are at work or at play. However, there is a strong devotion between the various brothers and sisters.

The existing companionship between the parents and

children is very commendable. Both boys and girls go to the father and mother for advice or consolation when they need it. The mother and daughter enjoy each other's company at work and on social occasions. The parents know their children's friends and make them welcome in the home. The mother often provides refreshments for a group of young people when they come to the house for an informal evening. However, some family discord is caused in the various homes by the varying closing hours of these gatherings as well as of planned socials. When one home has a conventional bedtime hour of eleven o'clock for the girl and she must stay at a party till after twelve, part of the pleasure of the evening is destroyed by the greeting which she gets when she arrives home. The girl has the use of the living room when her boy friends call and the son uses the family car when he goes to see a girl.

Family life is interrupted some by seasonal farm work, house cleaning, and butchering. During the potato harvest everybody works in a rush for long hours and there is little social life or recreation. Butchering time upsets the family for two or three days during the winter when the meat is put away, lard and sausage made and scrapple prepared. Usually one or two colored women are employed to help with this work.

The spring and fall house cleanings are the most upsetting events in the family routine. For a week or more the woman with the help of one or two hired women clean and rearrange the entire house. It is undertaken on a large scale and usually the woman abandons all civic or church work for the time being and merely provides food and clothes for the family. She gets very tired and the members of the family rejoice when the ordeal is over and the regular routine can be resumed. Friday is the weekly house-cleaning day and the woman seldom takes part in any activities outside of the home on that day.

The parents are willing for the children to practice the methods of farming and homemaking which they may learn at school and in 4-H club work. The parents themselves are quite up to date in their methods along these lines. They read quite a bit and listen to radio programs on various subjects. They also take advantage of information given by the farm and home demonstration agents.

The nature of potato culture, with a short growing season and brief harvest season, fair cash income in most years, family owned homes, and a fair division of labor among the various members of the family, is favorable for a well-regulated family life. Each person has a recognized place in the family and the family in turn has a place in the community. The mother has time to keep informed on current subjects and she trains her children in accepted standards of good manners and social graces.

The Out-of-School Girl

The parents kept the confidence of the daughter during the years in which a great part of her time was spent in school work. Her regular association from birth with relatives on family social occasions instilled in her many family customs and ideals which kept her close to the father and mother in her trend of thought. She has a cultural background and a deep appreciation of traditional family possessions. She has ideas and ideals of her own but they are based on those she inherited and she is not likely to be radical in her ideas of accepted standards of behavior.

She was sorry to leave school and begin a life of partial idleness when she had hoped to go to college or to train for some business or profession. She has several classmates and school friends in the community who were unable to carry out their plans after leaving school. She finished high school and probably took one year of post graduate work in commercial subjects. A few years before, all girls who wanted to could find work or go away to school. The older girls who went away to school made friends and visited in other states or counties and entertained these friends from a distance. The girls who finish high school now naturally aspire to similar experiences.

The girl left school with a depressed feeling for the goal of eleven or twelve years had been reached and she had no other immediate one to work for. After leaving school she realized her economic dependence which had never occurred to her while she was studying. She saw life differently from the way it looked while she was either studying or planning to return to her books at a definite date.

She helps with the housework in a general way but has little part in planning or managing the work or practice in spending the money. She gets no conception of the bigness of the job or the cost of operating a home. She may help a little with the harvest of the crop but this, too, is done in a general way without planning on her part.

This girl has a great deal of social life with her crowd and special boy friends. She has contacts, too, with young people from other places through church organizations. She belongs to such an organization but looks to three or four leaders to do most of the active work. She will go to movies, parties, dances, and other social events regularly.

She will likely become engaged to marry after three or four years of idleness. After the engagement she will direct her interests to a hope chest and trousseau. Several showers and parties will precede the home wedding. She will likely marry a boy she knew from childhood. He has a background of home life and education similar to hers, and they will live in the community and be a part of the younger set in which they grew up.

The disappointment of not having broad experiences in travel and in friends and acquaintances from other places may linger, but she will accept homemaking as her chosen vocation and put the best of herself into it. She may find the routine boresome as she develops skill and technique if there is not enough money to hire the work done, but she will follow the example of her mother and be a companion for her husband and make a home which the community will point to with pride.

CHAPTER IX

THE SUPERIOR RURAL FAMILY

EVERY community has one or more families who are recognized as leaders in civic, social, and financial activities. Living habits are influenced to some extent by local customs, but the superior family has individual characteristics regardless of the place of residence.

The family has a larger income, more property, a better house and furniture, more advanced education, and a better organized family life than the average in the community. The status of the family was inherited or gained by financial success which was used to raise the educational level and improve the social graces of the various members. The family usually lives for more than a generation in one community but the members take their accepted places in new communities when they change localities. The family is thrifty and provides a maximum of food and other necessities on the farm so that the cash income can be used to maintain a high living standard and to secure the advancement of the members.

PHYSICAL SURROUNDINGS

The house is designed to fit the architectural scheme of the locality and the needs of the family. There are usually two living rooms, dining room, kitchen, a bedroom for every two members of the family, and a provision for houseguests. The house has modern conveniences, such as lights, water, and a central heating plant. It is kept in good condition both outside and inside.

The furniture is artistic and comfortable and suited to the house or room in which it is used. Pleasing color schemes are worked out to suit the tastes of the various members of the family. Adequate storage facilities are provided for household equipment and personal articles of the various people living in the house.

The house is surrounded by a well-kept lawn, shade trees, and flowers. The garage and farm buildings are arranged at the back. Farm implements such as plows, rakes, axes, hoes, and shovels are carefully stored to prevent loss and deterioration by exposure to the weather. The farmstead is attractive in appearance, orderly, convenient, substantial, and homelike. All members of the family are proud of the home and willing to work for its improvement.

Outside Relations

The family has contacts with the community through the church, school, civic and social organizations, and special interest groups. However, since most of the contacts are in a leadership capacity, the family is not just one of the crowd. Personal friends are made among business associates, schoolmates, and relatives from towns or communities out of the immediate locality. The parents hold offices and teach Sunday-School classes in the church of their choice and the children take their places as leaders as they grow up. The parents keep in touch with the school and make complaints when standards are being lowered for they want their children to have the best opportunities the school can afford.

The man spends some time at the neighborhood gathering place, but business and improvements on his farm occupy a great deal of his time between crop seasons. He also goes to larger towns and to the county seat every few weeks.

The woman goes to a shopping center three or four times a month to buy household supplies. She takes a part in a woman's church organization and a social club in the community. She is also active in civic work. She has a profitable hobby and some regular form of recreation. She entertains her husband's business associates and their wives and attends social affairs in their circle.

The children form friendships with their classmates but seldom see them outside of school and church unless they are from superior families. Naturally the contacts the children have with people of their own age are limited. Their lack of experience because of limited associations sometimes makes them less capable of taking their places in a college group or in a new community as adults than children with fewer home advantages and more normal living with the neighborhood crowd.

Generally the family lives above petty quarrels and "falling outs" which are likely to exist in any community. The family is friendly with everybody but intimate with a select few, if any, of the neighbors. Usually the neighbors consider it an honor to receive any personal attention from the superior family either in church work, in time of need, or in a casual way.

Routine of Living

The superior family is so organized that the rights and opinions of all members are considered and the judgment of the parents is respected. Finances and other affairs relating to the family are openly discussed within the circle. But each member is taught to regard family matters as strictly private and not to mention them outside of the family. Servants who work in the home are taught to respect private affairs in the same way.

The household is operated in an efficient manner to provide physical comforts and social life for the family. The household is operated on a definite part of the annual income and provision is made for misfortunes. Investments or insurance policies provide for the maintenance of the family in case of death or disability of the wage earner.

The woman probably experimented a long time before arriving at a satisfactory way of handling the finances. If she began with no system and no knowledge of the cost of operating a house, she likely was disappointed when the bills came in and the husband complained about their size. If she attempted a strict budget system she likely found the bookkeeping boresome and was soon ready to abandon it. She probably adopted one in which all major expenditures were listed and a lump sum was allowed for incidentals. Then she and the man took equal parts or definite parts of the remainder to spend as they pleased without giving any account of how it was used. As the children grew up their share came out of this. Regardless of the system used the superior family avoids constant arguments about the use of the money. Having a definite sum to spend as he pleases, the man may treat his friends at the soda fountain without his wife labeling him extravagant. The woman is free to give a party and buy prizes if she chooses and to buy small household articles which the husband might think useless. A satisfactory way of handling the family finances whether the income is large or small probably solves half of the domestic troubles.

The system in use must give satisfaction to all members, for children in a family with a budget so rigid that it deprives them of things they want and other less fortunate children have, may become extravagant when they are free to spend as they please. The money must provide satisfaction as well as physical comforts and security in the future. The children are given responsibility in making personal purchases as they grow older. Each child has a weekly or monthly allowance which he must spend under guidance.

The woman does the housework with the help of other members of the family and probably a part-time maid. She does not feel it beneath her to cook or wash dishes when her compensation is appreciated by the people for whom she lives. She becomes attached to the china and silver and does not regard caring for it a burden since it is part of the equipment which makes a happy family life possible. The children are taught to appreciate the things the parents do for them and to enjoy doing things that other people appreciate.

Each member of the family has a specific job to do which is necessary for the efficient operation of the home.

The man and boys take care of all outside work such as milking the cows, caring for the chickens, working the garden, mowing the lawn, and bringing in the fuel. The girls have definite tasks which they are responsible for in the house. These tasks may be alternated so that the girl has the opportunity to learn all phases of housework. She is given managerial responsibility when she shows ability to take it.

The woman realizes the importance of keeping the family wardrobe in a good condition. She and the daughter do the laundry if such is the custom in the community, otherwise it is done by a washwoman. She realizes that being well-groomed gives poise and self-confidence, and is therefore willing to remodel clothes and to dry-clean them, if necessary, to make a good appearance on the available money.

As a rule the children are not paid for the work they do in the regular family routine but are taught that they are expected to contribute and that appreciation is the pay. Then they have a definite amount of money which is theirs because they are members of the family.

Everyday courtesies are observed in the family circle just as they are when important guests are present. The man uses the ash tray when he smokes, the boys rise when the mother enters the room, each person's bedroom is private unless he invites another in, mail is opened only by the owner, and well-modulated voices and gentle language are used.

The dining table is the family social center. Meals are served attractively and orderly and wholesome conversation accompanies them. The daughters take turns in serving so that the mother is free to direct the conversation and enjoy her food. Good table manners are observed at all times. Each member has an appetite for all dishes served in the balanced meals and eats without complaining or expressing his dislike of anything served. Holidays, anniversaries, and birthdays, are featured in the family dinners. Simple decorations or changes in the menu to carry out the spirit of the occasion adds interest and enjoyment. The family lives everyday for the happiness of its members and special preparation is unnecessary for guests other than increasing the amount of food and providing extra table space.

The family spends time in the evening reading, listening to music, and discussing current topics on which all members of the family keep informed. The family attends church socials, church services, school programs, and an occasional movie together. The various members attend special events apart from the family. The parents provide entertainment for the friends of the children when they come but the number entertained in the home is necessarily few.

If the family has maximum happiness and satisfaction in its private life, conflicts and differences which arise are settled immediately. Misunderstandings which leave those involved under a nervous tension can be detrimental to happiness. The superior family at its best makes each member feel that he is necessary for the happiness of others. Each one knows that his efforts in behalf of others are appreciated; he has an opportunity to express his ideas and hear those of others; each person gets inspiration and encouragement to do his best in his undertakings; there is someone to share the joys and sorrows which come into every life; and guidance is provided for the personal development of the members of the family through the sympathetic understanding of the group.

The Out-of-School Girl

The daughter of the superior family with her social heritage, educational advantages, and financial security may have a blighted social life which causes her to envy the average girl.

Likely the girl graduated from high school and went to college for one or more years. She discontinued the few friendships made in school. She made some new ones at college but probably found it hard to be just one of the crowd. However, she succeeded in making a few intimate friends whom she visited and entertained during her college days.

Upon her return home she found herself a stranger to the community and a partial stranger to her family, because of changed ideas and ideals in them and herself, but in different directions, during the separation. The mother is sympathetic with the girl and a companionship is soon renewed. The girl would like to go away and work but finds no job for which she has had training. She may not be interested in continuing the church work which she started as a young girl.

The girl has few contacts with girls and boys of her own age and interests. She feels that the crowd in the community is beneath her and she is far away from the friends she made in school. Therefore, she is likely to spend most of her time in an idle way with a disgusted feeling toward living because she cannot find the place to fill in life for which she had training. After a few idle months she is likely to be as restless and dissatisfied as the girl who left high school with the same disappointments. The parents are anxious for the girl to have social life but do not think the community crowd her equal. There are few others whom she sees regularly. So she must seek her companionship among older people.

This girl is likely to live an idle life and to get out of the habit of making a contribution to the community unless someone gets her back into the work just as soon as she returns to the community to stay. Since the girl in a superior family usually marries at a later age than the others, she could do a great deal of community work which would help her and the community before she becomes engaged. She has mentality, training, and ability which she uses very little beyond the family circle, and that is not broad enough to give her a satisfactory and well-rounded life.

CHAPTER X

INSTRUCTING THE GIRL IN THE FAMILY

THE FAMILY is the only institution to which the girl is directly responsible from the time she leaves school till she marries or works in a wage-earning capacity. This is the only time after early childhood that the family alone has claim on her. During this period the girl occupies a unique place in the home and community. This fact had little social significance when life was simple and the home had no competitors for the time and interests of women.

From the early part of the twentieth century till the United States entered the World War, few rural girls thought of forsaking the home to go out into the world and earn their own living. When the girl reached the age of eighteen, or before then, she quit the rural school to help with the housework and some field work. She pieced quilts, did fancywork, and learned to cook and sew. She was interested in some young man in the community and she realized that she must be skilled in household arts and possess a dozen or more quilts if she was to win his favor. She and her mother had a common interest in quilt making and needlework in general. The girl did not resent doing the housework exactly as her mother directed and she contented herself with the money the father gave her for clothes and other necessities. She accepted the family religion and the everyday routine of living without question or criticism.

When the United States entered the War, industry and business not only opened their doors to women but drafted them into service. Rural girls left home to work or to train for business or professional careers. During the following ten or twelve years most girls above sixteen years of age were able to find employment in a wage-earning capacity. The public schools offered additional advantages and college training and was possible for the more intelligent ones who wanted it. Higher education was idealized as the means to a job and a salary. In some cases the family would invest money in college training for the girl with the idea that she could soon return it and some extra to the family. If a girl expected to get married at an early date the family saw no need of higher education for her. When a teacher or social worker found an intelligent girl dissatisfied with her station in life, she urged her to finish school and get a job which would place her in a new environment.

The theory that removing the girl from her environment and placing her in a better one would make her happy did not always hold true. When she left home she usually gave up her friends or lost direct contact with them. If she lacked the personality to make new ones in a higher walk of life she was dissatisfied or very lonely. In some cases her salary was not large enough to provide both a satisfactory standard of living in her new environment and the financial contribution to the family that was expected of her. Moreover, she was sometimes embarrassed to introduce her new friends to the members of her family who had gone on in the same old rut. When the girl married, she probably kept her job and she and her husband adopted a standard of living which demanded the earnings of them both. When circumstances required her to give up her job, she was bewildered to try to maintain a home on a reduced income. However, she had the satisfaction of having earned her own living, of having contributed to the support of the family, and probably of having helped a brother or sister go to college.

The period of economic readjustment which began late in 1929 again changed the status of rural girls. The decline of business sent many of them back home as suddenly as the declaration of war had called them away. Girls who had earned their own money and contributed regularly to their families returned to financially depressed families without money or a chance to earn it. Some who had been trained for business or professions on borrowed money, and others who had been educated at a family sacrifice returned to become liabilities to their families again. This state of affairs caused a great deal of unrest till the girls replaced friends or relatives in jobs which they vacated to marry, or till the girls themselves married.

Each of the girls described in the preceding chapters is one of those who left school after the decline of business. She went through school with the idea of entering the business world and making her own living, but found the opportunity closed when she was ready either to take a job or to get advanced training. The more training she has the more she feels her disappointment in not having a chance to use it to earn an income, and the more disgusted she will be with an idle life.

Regardless of the community or the station in life in which the girl finds herself when she leaves school, the family is usually incapable of directing her in formulating a philosophy of life and a daily routine which will give her satisfaction and happiness during the late adolescent period. Educators accept the fact that there is a need for a guidance program for girls, but little research has been done and few attempts to work out a plan or program have been made.

The Home Economics Extension Service under the United States Department of Agriculture has taken the lead in developing a program for out-of-school girls. There are now organizations for these girls in several states. The groups in each state choose the name for such clubs. Some of the names are Junior Homemaker's Clubs, Senior 4-H Clubs, 4-H Service Clubs, and Utopia Clubs. Programs have been outlined to use as a guide in making plans for individual clubs. An effective program can be worked out with a particular group only after the leader is familiar with the background, experience, interests, and problems of the girls. The approach and working technique must be adapted to the individual community. Brief sketches of the work of three clubs in entirely different communities will illustrate some of the approaches which are being made to the problem:

CLUB WORK AMONG TOBACCO FARM GIRLS

A 4-H club of eleven girls and thirteen boys between the ages of sixteen and twenty-three was organized in a school district abandoned after consolidation in a tobacco farm community in January, 1930. All the members were in the same social class and several of the girls were interested in or engaged to boys in the club. One girl from a superior family and two from a dependent family did not accept the invitation to join the club.

Since both boys and girls worked in the field all day during the crop season, the meetings were held at night in the old schoolhouse. Both the farm and home demonstration agents, or capable leaders from outside of the community, attended each meeting. Separate groups for instructions in agriculture and homemaking projects were held during the first hour. A joint session followed in which six lessons on social customs were taught at six meetings by the home demonstration agent. Open discussions and demonstrations of principles involved occupied a great deal of the time in these periods. This was followed by a few minutes of recreation in which active games and group singing were featured. One benefit social, at which the club members presided as hosts and hostesses, was given to entertain the whole community.

Home visits and conferences with parents and prospective members preceded the organization of the group. When the agents were familiar with the needs and interests of the young people and had their confidence in what they had to offer, the tentative plans were explained to the local minister. Then a meeting was called, officers were elected, and a program of work was outlined by the agents and members in conference.

By the following September this organization was providing wholesome social and recreational activities, inspiration, vocational training, and social improvement for a group of overlooked young men and women.

CLUB WORK AMONG COAL MINE GIRLS

In October 1931 a home demonstration agent in a coal mining county interviewed a coal corporation manager regarding some extension work in his mining town. The office assistants listed eighteen out-of-school girls in the town of 400 inhabitants and the secretary accompanied the agent to talk with some of them. When the report of the visits was made, the corporation manager called the wife of the secretary and asked if she would be the leader for the girls and meet them once a week for home economics instruction and other activities which the home demonstration agent recommended. She consented to do this at the small salary he offered. An open discussion of the social facts of the girls was held in the conference of leaders and interested people so that the agent knew of illegitimacies, health conditions, family circumstances, and past records of all the girls. Only five were noticeably unadjusted by any of these causes.

Fourteen of the eighteen girls joined the club when the first meeting was called at the home of the secretary. The program was started with classes in which the girls made handicraft articles suitable for family Christmas presents and homemade candies. Then sewing lessons were given and the girls learned to make garments for themselves. A few minutes at each meeting were devoted to playing group games. Parliamentary rules were discussed and practiced in the meetings. Later, interest developed in social customs and in getting acquainted with the ways of communication and travel. A coöperative project was also selected.

A 4-H quilt was made by the girls and quilted by their mothers. The girls arranged the quilting party and served refreshments. The quilt was auctioned off and brought more than twenty dollars. This money started a fund which was used for socials and other club activities.

The club made a trip to a near-by large town to study the methods of travel and communication. They studied hotel customs, train courtesies, and behavior in public places. They also studied ways of packing bags for travel and the necessary equipment for overnight or longer trips. Arrangements were made for the club to visit the hotel. Each girl registered and the group went to a room where a formal meeting was held on travel customs. Telegrams were written and received, baggage checks presented, and railroad timetables studied. The girls ate in the hotel dining room and checked out of the hotel when it was time to leave.

Another trip included a visit to the newspaper office to see copies of the weekly paper printed. A few points on news writing as well as the technique of type-setting and printing were given by the editor of the paper.

Other activities of the club included a luncheon following a study of good table manners, a shower for one of the members who was to be married, and an evening party to which each girl invited a young man. The technique of entertaining was discussed in advance in each case, so that the social event was a demonstration of the principles learned.

This organization gave the girls a new interest in living and made them more anxious to conform to good standards of behavior than they had been in the past. They learned better methods of doing home work and that housekeeping could be made more than drudgery. They improved their personal appearance by making their own clothes rather than buying very cheap ones and by remodeling old ones. Within six months the club was making a noticeable and worthy contribution to the community.

CLUB WORK AMONG POTATO FARM GIRLS

A club of out-of-school girls in a potato farm community was organized in May 1933. Only high school graduates were invited to join the club. Fourteen girls became members of the club. They lived from a few yards to ten miles from the meeting place at the schoolhouse. Some of them had the use of the family car while others had to find other ways to go to the meetings.

These girls had a background of social graces and they were at home in any crowd. Their clothing standards were high enough for them to be inconspicuous with any well-dressed group. They all had some spending money and a reasonable amount of social life.

These girls chose a program of social service and recreation. Sewing for the local hospital was the first project. A great part of the time was devoted to recreation. Some of the girls had attended summer camps before money became scarce, so they talked a great deal about camp life.

During the summer plans were worked out for a beach party where the girls could carry their own food and do their work. In this way four days at camp cost very little. A cottage was rented, menus planned, each girl furnished with a list of groceries to bring, and a chaperon secured. Committees prepared the various meals so that nobody grew tired of cooking. One supper was prepared for invited guests. The girls invited their boy friends.

Swimming, dancing, singing, playing musical instruments, and handicrafts were the main features of the camp program. The girls learned that seashore recreation could be enjoyed at little cost; and they learned to prepare food in large quantities and to eat the things that were served. There was no choice in the menu for a hungry girl after a long swim.

This club gave the girls a chance to meet regularly although they lived some distance apart. School friendships were continued and worthwhile work was done in an organized way. The home demonstration agent and leader had an opportunity to know the girls intimately and to give them suggestions on personal problems when the girls asked for advice. The club reached girls in whom no other organization had a personal interest.

Each club served a definite need in the community for which it was planned. Anyone of the programs, however, would probably have been a failure among girls in another of the communities.

SUGGESTIONS FOR PROJECTS AND PROGRAMS

In addition to older girls' clubs some State Extension Departments are working out programs for the young men and women from sixteen to thirty years of age, through county and community organizations patterned after the Youth Section of the American Country Life Association. The subjects included in such programs are: Recreation and Culture, Civic Improvement and Citizenship, Ethics and Religion, Rural Home and Family Life, Rural Government and Public Welfare. One county in the potato section of Virginia included in its program of recreational and cultural subjects for the first year dramatics, vocal and instrumental music, public speaking, chemistry, handicrafts, and writing. Young people interested in a particular subject were located through various contests, sponsored by a committee of leading young people guided by the county extension workers and state extension sociologist. The first project was a short story contest. Announcements of this were made through the county papers and churches. Cash prizes were donated by local civic organizations and the awards were made at a banquet. The three winners in the contest became a standing committee to promote story and news writing in the county.

A strong social and recreational program for the out-of-school girl usually makes an appeal which holds the members. As the years after leaving school increase the social contacts decrease. A study in one county showed that the out-of-school girls had less than two-thirds as many invitations to parties, picnics, and other social gatherings as those near the same age in school.

Many conflicts arise when one attempts to direct a program of social activities for young people of several social levels during the courting age. Therefore, selecting the crowd has to be left to a great extent to the girls themselves, with enough direction by the leader to prevent the club from becoming merely a social clique, excluding those who most need some guidance from outside the home.

Certain city community centers have worked out programs for the girls of the out-of-school class with activities including their boy friends. In one place any crowd can have a club at the community center if enough young people ask for it. Only people approved by the crowd starting the club can belong. If a strange girl comes to the center, she must make friends outside of the club and be invited to join before she is admitted. This method of selecting the group is not practical in the rural community because the young people are not especially anxious to organize and there are not enough available members to have special friendship groups.

No one method of organizing a club is likely to work in several communities and the program will probably have to be planned to meet each need. In some cases the social activities may have to be limited to the girls only. This is especially true where boy friends of some of the girls are considered undesirable by parents of other members. These social problems will have to be studied by the leader, conflicts avoided when possible and settled when they do arise.

The program projects will have to be chosen with discretion if they are to challenge and hold the interest of the majority of the girls. Their home backgrounds are different and their educational advantages vary. Some probably had home economics training and others did not. Therefore, a choice of activities, or required work will be necessary. The subjects studied should have some relation to each girl's immediate experiences for she is little interested in the future. If she lives in a community where people are interested in antique furniture, old china, colonial architecture, and formal gardens, a study of these with social tours to observe some of them may have an appeal; but these subjects would not interest the girl who knows bungalow houses and modernistic furniture. Studies of these articles in the form the girls know them, with visits to local furniture stores or to well-furnished homes in the community, may interest any girl. She is usually interested in her own room, and therefore furniture principles, rug making, and good housekeeping practices may be taught through her interest in the room. Pictures, music, and literature may be made interesting if directly connected with the girl's everyday experiences.

Dramatics and community singing usually interest out-of-school girls. Programs centered around these subjects can include the boys. They can be worked out for community entertainment and money-making schemes as well as for providing the young people with enjoyable organized recreation. Often the best dramatic talent in the high school class is discarded when a girl graduates, and her overworked younger sister struggles along trying to take part in school plays to make money while the more talented girl is longing for something interesting to do.

A review of any domestic relation court record furnishes evidence that women need to know more about the laws under which they live. Misunderstandings about the status of children in unadjusted homes, temporary foster parents, property rights of women and children, and problems of non-support could probably be decreased if women knew their legal status in the matter. A study of current happenings of this sort which can be lifted above petty gossip can make an appeal to girls who may want to go deeply into the state laws regarding the rights of the family.

Health education has a direct relation to the girl's everyday life. By coöperation with local health units a program on this subject can often be worked out which leads to needed correction of physical defects and to the prevention of future suffering.

A study of the lives of girls in other lands, as well as those of girls of other occupations in our own country, may interest the girl in analyzing her own family life. Reviews of biographies of American women and stories of home and family life may give girls a vision of a better organized family than the one they grew up in. If they become students of family life, they can absorb many points of good management or organization as they visit relatives and friends. They can also detect points which lead to clashes and unhappiness.

Some girls may be interested in making booklets which give a summary of each meeting. These may grow into pleasant hobbies and may be expanded to include the girl's dream home with house furnishings, ideal husband, and family organization. However, the exceptional girl will be interested enough to carry her study to this extent. Like the classroom teacher, or the garment maker, the girl is more likely to make a successful home if she has a pattern to go by or a goal to reach than if she attempts it with no definite aim or ideal in mind.

Every girl desires to be a gracious hostess and to take her place at social functions. Débutantes get a great deal of practice in this phase of life during their out-of-school period and other girls get it at exclusive schools. This practice gives them poise in the social circles in which they are to live. Since the rural girl has the same desire to be at home in the best circles of her community, she can profit by practice in simple entertaining on the level in which her crowd will find its amusement in the future. Therefore, a study of social gatherings, etiquette of each, and ways of entertaining on an inexpensive scale will probably appeal to most girls.

In Denmark apprenticeship in a well-organized home after classroom activities are finished is a part of the public school training. And, according to press reports, work camps have been established in Germany to provide training in the mechanics of homemaking for girls after they finish school. So far only girls seeking relief have gone to them, but a law is being advocated to require every girl to take a year of such training. Girls so trained may get practical experience by taking charge of homes for a few weeks while tired homemakers attend a work camp or take a vacation.

In comparison, the American girl has a great many

more educational advantages than the Danish girl, and probably greater freedom in selecting her course of study than the German girl, but the public school leaves her only partly trained for life. The world pities a girl who marries a man incapable of making a living, but only the negro mammy is known even to sympathize with a man who marries a girl ignorant of the technique of housekeeping. The American public has taken for granted the fact that homemaking ability is either hereditary or acquired naturally. This theory does not hold true when the duty of the home is to help readjust the economic and social unrest of the world today.

A program of transitional education for the girl from the time she leaves school until she is in her own home should give her practice in the elementary principles of housekeeping, skill and efficiency in minimizing undesirable physical labor, and confidence in her ability to do things right. A partnership between the mother and her daughter may be worked out whereby the daughter can have practice in all phases of housework and management of the home under methods learned at school or in the after-school program. If the girl is not permitted to use her home economics training from the day she passes her last examination till she is married, she will probably forget most of the things she has learned.

The supply of possible subject matter for the out-of-school program for rural girls is unlimited, but the subject taught is merely the means to an end far more important. The program should help the girl form a philosophy of life which will lead her to be contented with her station in life and to make a worthwhile contribution to the community through her home and through outside activities. During the late adolescent period her ideas and ideals are changing and developing. A few months of idleness may cause her to develop a habit of restlessness and dissatisfaction with living which will follow her the rest of her life. In her idle search for excitement she may meet with calamities which will permanently handicap her in making the proper adjustments to society as a whole. Since the public has provided formal education for the girl for eleven years or less, surely its responsibility should extend over the hardest years of her life, the years in which the parents are usually less qualified to take the whole responsibility of inspiring and directing her.

The Agricultural and Home Economics Extension Service is probably the best qualified organization to carry out a program of transitional education for rural young people. The nature of the program in general is based on existing needs and is flexible enough to meet changing needs. The present system provides for clubs for young people from fifteen to twenty years of age, in addition to the regular 4-H clubs. If the program is of such a nature as to hold the young people after they leave school, and if a large number of those who remain at home can be included, the problem will be fairly simple. The Extension personnel is limited and the public has already learned to expect a great many things from the workers, so that finding sufficient time to devote to an intensive program of work for the older young people will be difficult. Moreover, the number of youth-minded leaders available either as paid workers or volunteers is limited in the rural community.

The need for an educational program for the "Girl in the Rural Family" is evident, and surely providing guidance for her from school to her own home is just as much a public obligation as making a common school education available. Regardless of the organization which assumes the responsibility of undertaking this new form of education, the problem is important enough to merit the co-operation of the home, the school, the church, and every other social agency in any rural community.

www.ingramcontent.com/pod-product-compliance
Lightning Source LLC
Chambersburg PA
CBHW030118010526
44116CB00005B/298